Collateral Damage

A Journey in Dealing with Combat-related PTSD

GEORGE M. COEN

DEDICATION

In the beginning was the Word,
and the Word was with God,
and the Word was God.
He was with God in the beginning.
Through him all things were made;
without him nothing was made that has been made.
In him was life, and that life was the light of all mankind.
The light shines in the darkness and the darkness has not overcome it.

— John 1: 1-5 (NIV)

Acknowledgements

In December of 2016, during one of my therapy sessions with Dr. Laird, the subject of yoga came up as a helpful tool in one's quest for presence of mind and relaxation. This led me to Melody Madonna, who operated a local yoga studio specializing in Iyengar yoga techniques. She also had a very extensive book collection. Melody and her husband, Joe Hutchison had at one time operated a used book store.

Mr. Hutchison was Colorado's Poet Laureate 2014–2018, had published 17 books, and taught at the University of Denver. In my first conversation with him I told him about a book I wanted to write but didn't know how to get started. He offered two pieces of advice; First, I should read Mary Karr's book, *The Art of Memoir*, and second, "I should write what was on my mind."

Since then, this project has involved countless other individuals to whom I am indebted and grateful to:

To my wife, Donna, and our four children who have all taken part in various ways—from inspiration, to critical review and comment. Thank you for your support and encouragement.

To my friends and associates that took part in discussion, critique, review, and collaboration which kept me on track and accountable, you have my utmost thanks and appreciation.

To the many participants in my life story, some whom I have been able to name, Thank you for being there.

To my caregivers, who over the years were part of my team and recovery, I hope I have made you proud of what you do and who you are. Thank you!

And last, but not least, to my shipmates—you know who you are—those alive, those who sacrificed, and those who have passed on. It has been my honor to have served and shared a part of my life with you. Thank you and may God bless you!

CONTENTS

PREFACE

This is not a story about the war—my war, my father's war, his father's war, or your war.

This is a story about healing—physical, mental, and spiritual.

This story is about warriors and the wounds they suffered from war, primarily those of a physiological nature. Those wounds, in many cases, were then inflicted upon others who became indirect war victims.

This is a story about those wounds. This is a story about a few warriors and how they have dealt with their wounds—some seeking treatment, some not.

This is a story about the treatment process and the caregivers who are a part of that process.

This is a story about hope, accomplishment, and a future.

This is also a story about reality. The reality that treatment doesn't always mean cure, the reality that treatment may mean acceptance of reality, and learning to manage and cope with that reality.

This is a story about opportunity through acknowledgement, education, and acceptance of an altered mental health condition resulting from uninvited exposure to trauma.

This story begs acknowledgement of conditions and events outside of the experienced trauma that can significantly influence the presence and severity of behavioral reactions, which can become diagnosed as trauma-related disorders or symptoms.

My part of this story involves growing up with a father who suffered severe diagnosed but untreated combat-related PTSD. I later experienced combat-related trauma myself—again, diagnosed and untreated—and then, 40 years later, experienced a subsequent severe trauma. The cumulative effect of these events, not uncommon in many households of today, left a trail of negative impacts—not only to me, but to countless other unsuspecting individuals, a punishment undeserved.

The unfortunate irony is that if there had been appropriate recognition, alteration of behaviors, and/or treatment, a great deal of pain and disruption could have been avoided.

The lasting effects of trauma, of whatever nature, are real. Labeling and stigmatizing the resulting symptoms is not helpful or productive. Education and treatment, sometimes prolonged, can help. While a cure for symptoms is elusive, treatment can temper the severity of symptoms; and survivors can not only find some degree of normalcy, but also thrive.

This story is about finding peace for one's soul.

INTRODUCTION

In 1967, I was discharged from the U.S. Navy after serving a three-year enlistment. I was 30 days short of my 21st birthday, still under the age to legally purchase alcohol in the United States.

During my three-year enlistment, I served two deployments to the Vietnam theater as part of a Navy attack squadron assigned to the aircraft carriers *Ticonderoga* and *Enterprise*. For the majority of these deployments, I carried out my assigned duties as part of the squadron's flight deck personnel.

Within 30 days of my separation from the Navy, I became ill and, as instructed, reported to the local Veterans Administration Hospital in Albuquerque, New Mexico. Following medical examination, which included a general physical exam and an "upper GI" procedure, I was diagnosed as having anxiety reaction, ulcers, and significant high-frequency hearing loss. I was given some antacid medicine, anti-anxiety medication, and a recommendation to seek a private-sector medical provider for any further needs. I subsequently received a VA disability rating for all three ailments.

For the next 37 years I continued to suffer from the mental and physical effects of "chronic anxiety." Startle response and hypervigilance were just part of my regular life. In 2004, I experienced a subsequent traumatic event, which resulted in a significant aggravation of my existing neurological symptoms. A private-sector psychiatrist diagnosed me as having post-traumatic stress disorder (PTSD).

PTSD is an anxiety disorder that some people get after seeing or living through a dangerous event. When in danger, it's natural to feel afraid. This fear triggers many split-second changes in the body to prepare to defend against the danger or to avoid it. This "fight or flight" response is a healthy reaction meant to protect a person from harm. In people with PTSD, this reaction is changed or damaged. "People who have PTSD may feel stressed or frightened even when they're no longer in danger."[1]

1 Frequently Asked Questions about Post-Traumatic Stress Disorder (PTSD)–Brain & Behavior Research Foundation

"PTSD was first officially recognized as a mental health condition in 1980, five years after the end of the Vietnam War. For hundreds of years, these symptoms have been described under different names in soldiers from many wars. However, Vietnam Veterans with these symptoms were the first to have the term 'PTSD' applied to them. Despite the passage of 50 years since the war, for some Vietnam Veterans, PTSD remains a chronic reality of everyday life. In 1983, Congress requested that the VA conduct a study on the prevalence of PTSD and other postwar psychological problems among Vietnam Veterans. This was the first study to evaluate the prevalence of PTSD among veterans and became known as the National Vietnam Veterans Readjustment Study (NVVRS). The NVVRS brought greater attention to the issue of PTSD as it found that as many as 15 percent of veterans had PTSD."[2]

Symptoms of PTSD include:

1. ***Reliving the event***
   Unwelcome memories about the trauma. ... This is called a flashback and may include nightmares. Memories of the trauma can happen because of a trigger— something that reminds you of the event ... hearing a car backfire might bring back memories of gunfire for a combat veteran.

2. ***Avoiding things that remind you of the event***
   A combat Veteran may avoid crowded places like shopping malls because it feels dangerous to be around so many people.

3. ***Having more negative thoughts and feelings than before***
   You may feel that the world is dangerous, and you can't trust anyone. It may be hard for you to feel or express happiness, or other positive emotions.

4. ***Feeling on edge***
   It's common to feel jittery or "keyed up"—like it's hard to relax. This is called hyperarousal. You might have trouble sleeping or concentrating or feel like you're always on the lookout for danger. You may suddenly get angry and irritable—and if someone surprises you, you might startle easily.
   ... Here's the good news: you can get treatment for PTSD.
   ...For some people, treatment can get rid of PTSD altogether. For others, it can make symptoms less intense. Treatment also gives you the tools to manage symptoms, so they don't keep you from living your life.[3]

---

2 PTSD and Vietnam Veterans: A Lasting Issue 40 years Later–www.public health.va.gov
3 National Center for PTSD–Understanding PTSD and PTSD Treatment February 2018

In 2005 I found myself part of this population. I sought treatment for conditions which had now become significant enough that my ability to function effectively in a workplace environment was almost impossible.

For the next three years, I diligently sought out private-sector medical providers who had knowledge of this condition. During this period, I was examined and treated by no less than 20 separate medical or neurological providers. Treatment included drug prescriptions of about every available SSRI (selective serotonin reuptake inhibitor). I found I was unable to tolerate these SSRIs in any significant dosage. Besides drug therapy, I underwent a 40-session hyperbaric chamber treatment protocol, EMDR therapy, neurofeedback training, e-stem therapy, as well as numerous psychotherapy sessions.

With little to show for results, one of my providers suggested that I should contact the Veterans Administration regarding my condition.

With the Disabled American Veterans organization acting as my advocate, and following extensive examination and testing, in 2011 the Veterans Administration formally acknowledged my PTSD condition as service-connected and agreed to undertake its treatment.

Since that time, I have been in continuous treatment under the care of the VA Eastern Colorado Health Care System, Golden, Colorado Clinic Mental Health Facility. My PTSD is by no means cured, but I have successfully learned how to manage my symptoms.

The Veterans Administration road, by itself, has taken over 7 years to get to my current state. I still suffer significant symptoms, but I am now able to function with some semblance of normalcy, most of the time.

The story of my long road to recovery cannot be told without including my childhood, which also must include some mention of previous generations who were part of my development process. As you will see, PTSD began affecting me long before I went to war.

MY FATHER'S WAR

My paternal grandfather, George E. Coen, was born somewhere in Ohio in October 1892. I know little about his younger years.

I do know that he and his brother Bill enlisted in the Navy (grandpa was underage at the time), and they served together aboard a battleship. I believe the two of them participated in Teddy Roosevelt's "around-the-world tour." Both visited Odessa, and they were at Constantinople long enough for Bill to meet and marry Jeanne.

Grandpa was a baker in the Navy. He had flat feet and wore arch supports; this was apparently discovered by a young ensign, who threw the arch supports over the side. When grandpa made sick call to try and replace them, he was at once invalided out of the Navy.

He met my grandmother, Marie Mae Doutaz, in Kentucky, where he worked as a mechanic. They were married and then went to Canada selling enlarged portraits. During this time, they had three children, who were born just south of the Canadian border. My Dad, George F., was born in 1917 in Oil City, Pennsylvania.

Grandpa worked as a salesman for a Ford agency. In the fall of 1923, Grandpa got some financing and moved to Deshler, Ohio, where he started a Chevrolet agency.

The Depression forced Grandpa out of business in 1931, and the family moved to Montpelier, Ohio.

Between 1929 and 1932, my dad's life was very tenuous as his mother, Marie, was suffering from a hyperactive thyroid gland. Grandpa arranged for an operation, but at the last minute she refused to go through with the surgery. Violence became more and more the order of the day, and my father and grandfather were increasingly in fear. (Insane violence is said to be one of the results of thyroid problems.) At some point my grandmother was committed to the state hospital at Lima for several months.

Grandpa took over a Chevrolet agency in Montpelier, Ohio. My father attended the Montpelier High School for his sophomore year. The business folded, and they moved to Fort Wayne, Indiana, in 1932.

By this time the family had split. Grandpa and Marie divorced. Grandpa and my dad lived together in Fort Wayne. Dad attended South Side High School and was halfway through his senior year when they moved to Warsaw, Indiana.

My dad graduated from Warsaw High in May 1934. By then, Grandpa was in Indianapolis at the Oldsmobile agency. My dad joined him after graduation, and they lived in the suburb of Ravenswood on the east bank of the White River. Dad was only 16 and small for his age.

Dad worked summers in the grocery in Ravenswood and wintered as a migrant worker in the fields. He bought a bicycle, put a bedroll on it, and ranged from Michigan to Texas, migrating with the wind as the seasons came on. Summers he spent in Ravenswood. By 1936 Grandpa had remarried and acquired three stepchildren, two sons and a daughter. They lived in Little Rock, Arkansas. My father was unable to put down roots there; he worked in a factory in Indianapolis and lived in Ravenswood.

Dad Becomes a Soldier

In 1938, dad believed that he was going to be involved in a war. He learned to shoot, and in April of 1940 returned to Little Rock, joined the 153rd Infantry, and waited to be mobilized. The 153rd was called up in December of 1940 and in August 1941 was sent to Camp Murry, near Tacoma, Washington. When the war opened after Pearl Harbor, the 153rd was detailed to guard duty at nearby McCord Field.

Dad spent his evenings and some weekends studying at Camp Murry, regardless of the fact that they were at a port of embarkation and expected to leave at any moment. Dad wanted to be a navigator, so he studied physics and mathematics. He tried to volunteer for the Air Corps, but they were not interested in him in November 1941.

By February 1942 the Air Corps had changed the requirements for training from four years of college to the ability to pass a test.

Dad walked out of the test at half time, knowing that he had done well. He went to the Tacoma Public Library to thank one of his friends and mentors, Miss Clara Van Sant, for her help with his studies. By the time he got back to the base (he had spent several hours enroute) the first sergeant spotted him and called him over. He came to attention, with some apprehension, whereupon the first sergeant said, "Coen we've heard from Fort Lewis, and you are not to leave the USA."

He shortly received orders to report to Santa Ana Army Air Base, where he was put into the class of 42-13. When he first arrived at Santa Ana he took the Stanine battery of tests and was classified as a pilot. He went to the tactical officer and said that he would not make a good pilot, but that he would be a first-rate navigator. The tactical officer shook his head sadly and made the change on his clipboard.

After three months at Santa Ana, In June 1942, his class was sent to Mather Field at Sacramento for navigation training. He was commissioned a second Lieutenant in September 1942 and was sent to Salt Lake City, where he was assigned to the Second Air Force.

On September 25, 1942, the 99th Bombardment Group (Heavy) was activated at Gowan Field near Boise, Idaho. Colonel Faye R. Upthegrove was designated as the Group Commander, and Lieutenant Colonel Leroy A. Rainey was designated as the deputy Group Commander. The 99th consisted of the 346th, 347th, 348th and 416th Bomb squadrons. Due to congestion at Gowan Field, the 99th immediately relocated to Walla Walla, Washington. During October, the 99th received twelve flight leaders with crews, and four B-17 Flying Fortress bombers. During the first phase of training, the 99th received six more B-17s. The winter weather in Washington was not favorable for flying, so the 99th relocated to Sioux City, Iowa, for the second phase of training. By the middle of November, the 99th had acquired about seventy-five percent of its ground and support personnel. The third phase of training took place at Salina, Kansas, in mid-January of 1943.[4]

Dad had asked for combat, and that was what he got. After three days, he was sent to Boise, Idaho, where the 99th Heavy Bombardment Group was being formed. His crew—Cardwell, Imrie, Bulkeley, Willoughby, Bradfute, Buxton, Litwalk, and Shelnutt—was formed. Cardwell was replaced by a guy named Henderson from Lufkin-on-the-pipeline, Texas. After a month at Boise they were sent to Walla Walla, Washington; thence to Sioux City, Iowa—where they flew as a crew, also as a squadron, and even as a group—moving then to Salina, Kansas. Henderson went over to the Boeing plant and returned with B-17 #229502.

---

4 99th Bomb Group Historical Society–Thunder from The South, History of the 99th Bombardment Group

At Salina, Kansas, B-17 #229502 became known as BTO (Big-time Operator). They then began briefings for overseas flight. Planes were loaded up with clean shirts and whiskey and other essentials; they then flew to Deridder, Louisiana, for training in overwater flying. By then there were only 35 crews in the 99th of the 36 formed at Boise. The final U.S. embarkation point was Morrison Field at West Palm Beach, Florida.

In November of 1942, Allied forces under the command of General Dwight D. Eisenhower, based in Gibraltar, began what was labeled as Operation Torch. Allied troops landing in French North Africa, Oran, and Algiers began their assault eastward with the intention of isolating and defeating German General Rommel and his Afrika Korps, who were successfully battling for control of North Africa with eyes on the Suez Canal.

Isolation required cutting all air and sea resupply lines to Rommel coming from German-occupied Italy and France. As planned, following the eastward-advancing army ground forces, strategic airfield assets in North Africa would be occupied. From these bases, strategic air operations could be undertaken north across the Mediterranean. The plan was to cripple or destroy the German-occupied, French resupply infrastructure.

By the spring of 1943, this operation was well underway, and United States Army Air Corp assets began mobilizing from the United States to North Africa.

After completion of overwater training, the 99th departed the United States at Morrison Field in February. The 99th B-17s flew the southern route via Boriniquen, Puerto Rico; Georgetown, British Guiana; Belem, Brazil; Bathhurst, Gambia; to their destination at Marrakech, Morocco. The ground and support personnel and equipment made the journey by ship.[5]

After less than 12 months of training, my father was going to receive his wish; he was headed to war as a commissioned second lieutenant, and a B-17 navigator. I do not know what his thoughts may have been as he guided his squadron south to Brazil, then across the mid-Atlantic to Gambia, and back north to Morocco. He was a soldier, serving his country without question, the legitimacy of the operation not his to question. Like most airmen of that generation, I believe he had little expectation for his own survival and certainly no consideration for his own personal condition in the unlikely event he should survive.

---

5 99th Bomb Group Historical Society–Thunder from The South–History of the 99th
   Bombardment Group

Combat in Dad's Own Words

Some forty years later, as a weary and battle-scared veteran, my father did take some time to reflect and record his memories of those 50 combat missions over North Africa, Sicily, Italy, and France. At that point, in the late 1980s, PTSD was yet to be a recognized affliction, but he was certainly a victim. The forty years following his repatriation were ample evidence of that.

Here is part of his story as he remembered it forty years later.

> *We lifted off for our flight across the Atlantic and eventually North Africa, via Puerto Rico, British Guiana, and—but I better tell more about British Guiana.*
>
> *The fields were in the process of being lengthened and stumps removed. They were all short, so we had to use brakes a lot. Punjab Imrie (Co-Pilot) must have set the brakes when we were at the top of a bounce, and we wore off twenty plies and coated the flaps with rubber. We were immobilized until tires could be flown in to us. Lacking barracks accommodations, the Permanent Party put our whole crew in the venereal disease ward, which made us so mad that we went out and lived in the plane. I borrowed a jeep and several of us went out to the end of the road where the Indios[6] brought in little red bananas in their dugout canoes. The Indias[7] liked Punjab's looks a lot. I traded a quart of whiskey for a can of tuna fish to a friend from Indiana who was a cook there.*
>
> *While making our way southeastward along the coast of Brazil at about 4,000 feet altitude I had the nose of the plane all to myself. The nose also contained various luggage in order to balance the plane. The plane was heavily laden with such items as a big tow bar. It obviously handled a bit sluggishly. Consequently, when the plane suddenly nosed over and dove for the shallow seas off the coast of Brazil, I doubted that we could get it back into level flight without tearing off the wings. As the air speed went well beyond the red line and kept creeping upward I decided to stand there and enjoy my last minute or two. Below us were sharks, crocodiles, and hostile Indios. We had lost crews in that Mato Grosso[8] who could not be reached for rescue. They could be kept alive by parachute drops until the Indios reached them and mashed their heads.*
>
> *While the waves were getting closer, up on the flight deck the pilots were pushing themselves off the ceiling into their seats so as to fasten their seat belts and begin hauling back on the control yoke to pull the plane out of that deadly dive. They succeeded although we were perilously near the muddy waves. Had we gone in nobody would have known what happened to us.*

---

6 A member of any of the indigenous peoples of America or eastern Asia in areas formerly subject to Spain or Portugal.
7 Feminine tense of *Indio*.
8 Mato Grosso, a large state in west-central Brazil, is mostly covered with Amazon rainforest, wetlands, and savanna plains.

Presently Bombardier Bulkeley came down into the nose and began removing luggage to get at the bombsight, presumably to revise the setting of the automatic pilot which had betrayed us. Neither Bulkeley nor the two pilots had any memory of this event in 1989, but I sure remember it.

Eventually we got to Belem Brazil, thence to Natal Brazil the eastern most point in South America, for our Atlantic crossing.

We flew the Atlantic at night. Nobody saved any sandwiches for the navigator, so I was pretty hungry when we finally found Yundum, Gambia near Bathurst (Banjul), and landed.

Henderson made a rough landing on the roller-coaster steel mat and then asked Willoughby, (the radioman) "Can you get the tower for me, I cannot raise them." Willoughby shoved forward with the radio in his arms where the landing had shaken it from its rack on the fuselage and said, "Here it is, get them yourself."

Bulkeley and I went together to the mess hall where a British soldier told a tall African cook "Two chop." The cook wiped his hands on a filthy apron. I said, "One chop" and bolted for the door. The can of tuna tasted delicious. We engaged two native guides of about eight years age. Their names were Omar and Kevodovich. I remember only the cattle egrets, the large vultures, and the baboons. We lifted off for Marrakech, Morocco after a day or two, and my last memories are of the workers (who were lengthening the runway) running for safety as the old BTO chewed her way through the palm trees.

The 99ᵗʰ was attached to the 5ᵗʰ Bombardment Wing of 12ᵗʰ Air Force. The 12ᵗʰ Air Force was stationed at Navarin, North Africa, located near Constantine.

We arrived at Tafaraoui, Algeria airport in early March 1943. The place was pretty badly beaten up by allied bombers and had the worst bedbugs and the worst mud in Africa. We soon lifted off for La Senia, Algeria where the Mediterranean monsoon kept us grounded. We went out daily to turn over the engines of the BTO, and daily I plodded by an old buried latrine which had the name of the outfit on it. Gradually it soaked into my skull that the outfit named was that of my step brother Jack West. I stepped into the orderly tent and inquired about him, I was told "oh you mean Pappy." We had a good reunion, and when we took the BTO up to slow-time a new engine, we took Jack along. Alas, the engine had to be feathered at once (reportedly because the rings were in backward) and we proceeded to bomb the target range in the Sebkret d' Oran on three engines. This did not thrill Jack at all. We landed and removed the engine. Meanwhile, the skies cleared and the 99ᵗʰ went up towards Kasserine Pass. The Germans had pushed our men back when the skies were stormy, but in clear weather we could send out the heavies (that's the B-17s) to discuss the situation. We got the new engine, but by that time there was a foot of water on the runway as the storms returned. When the runway at La Senia was cleared, the runway at the 99ᵗʰ's post was still soaked, and since that runway was dirt, we could not land on it.

The 99ᵗʰ flew its first combat mission on March 31,1943. The 99ᵗʰ came to be referred to as the Diamondbacks, due to a diamond insignia painted on the vertical stabilizer of their B-17s. As Allied ground forces forced the German Afrikakorps to retreat into Tunisia, the 12ᵗʰ Air Force flew missions to cut off German supplies coming from Italy and Sicily. For the rest of 1943, the 99ᵗʰ flew missions primarily across the Mediterranean Sea to bomb targets in Sicily and Italy.

In June, news of a possible Arab uprising had the men of the 99ᵗʰ nervous and wearing side arms at all times. Although a major uprising never occurred, there were acts of sabotage; including a small night time paratrooper drop over Oudna Field, Tunisia that resulted in the capture of three Germans.

Summer dust storms made life miserable. On July 5ᵗʰ, the group bombed an airfield at Gerbini, Sicily. An estimated one hundred enemy fighters made repetitive and fierce attacks, trying to turn the 99ᵗʰ back. The group however penetrated enemy defenses and destroyed the airfield. For this mission, the 99ᵗʰ received its first Distinguished Unit Citation. On July 9ᵗʰ, the group flew missions in support of the Allied invasion of Sicily. The first Allied air attack on Rome took place on July 14ᵗʰ. Great care was taken by the 99ᵗʰ to avoid dropping any bombs on the Vatican City."⁹

Our plane and crew finally caught up with our buddies of the 416ᵗʰ Bombardment Squadron, 99ᵗʰ Bomb group, at a little village known as Mechtat Oulad Hamdu five kilometers southwest of St. Arnaud, Algeria. The wide dirt runways at an elevation of 4,000 feet and a Latitude of 36-60 were on the north edge of the Sahara where caravans came through the mountains. Nearby lakes were very nearly flat, perhaps one foot of depth and two miles wide. Djebel Oulad Hamdu was a basalt mesa about one-half square mile in area. There was a thirst parlor in St. Donat.

After the arrival of the BTO at Notary, as all our fields were known to the military, the rains resumed. The fine-grained soils when dry was like iron, but when wet would not support a plane with engine running. The vibration of a running engine would cause the plane to sink into the hardstand to the hubs, so we got a welcome rest while allowing the African sun to dry out the field. While occupied, we were visited by the 2ⁿᵈ Bomb Group, newly arrived in the theater. The CO of the second was a classmate of Colonel Upthegrove, (Uppie), so the second came over in impressive formation, wheeled, and began to form into landing pattern, strung out in a line. Meanwhile our radio was begging them not to land, but they were not in tune and did not hear the message.

Plane Number One landed, plowing two enormous ruts into our nicely manicured field. Plane Number Two plowed enormous ruts into the other side of the runway. Plane Number Three saw the mess in time to advance throttles and get back up into the air, and the 2ⁿᵈ Bomb went on to their original destination.

9 99th Bomb Group Historical Society–Thunder from The South–History of the 99th Bombardment Group

Our Crew began Operation Torch combat operations with a little political discussion at Trapani, Italy, on the island of Sicily, in which we destroyed so many Axis aircraft that HQ insisted they had to be dummies. Fortunately, we had picked up a photographer at Oran and could substantiate our claim. This set the stage for what is now known as "the Palm Sunday Massacre", which you can read about in "ROMMEL'S LAST STAND". As we came off the target I thought to myself "O ye squareheads, while you are making a meal, I'm going to get a bite!" I was by then known as Trigger Coen, The Arkansas Traveler, and the name was painted on my astrodome. I had wisely resisted efforts to nickname me "Killer Coen." That would have been difficult to explain to jurymen later in my peaceful career.

While enroute across the South Atlantic I had no chance to draw pay until arrival in Morocco. When we arrived there, we were able to draw our pay in francs. The two months' arrears of pay were earned at a time when the franc was valued at one cent, but by the time we were able to draw our pay the Big Boys had decided that two cents per franc would be even better, so I drew an extra two months' pay, fourteen months in all that year. My faith in a managed currency declined from that day.

I later discovered Coen's Currency coefficient, the lower limit of value below which a currency cannot go. When the lovely engraved notes have reached the same value as toilet paper, they will stay at that value for an unknown time.

Out of respect for chivalry, I rendered the salute "Heil Hitler" from time to time. The occasion would always be when I was swinging my machine gun onto a second target, and I may have omitted both the words and motions, but the chivalry was there!

I swore at the first German with whom I negotiated, called him a son of a bitch, but thereafter I kept myself under better control and never said anything defamatory of our honorable opponents.

The month of April 1943 was rainy. The 99th stood by to drop leaflets or something on Rommel's tankers. We were usually relieved from duty about 10 am and could steal a jeep and go get drunk. The exact details of this R&R are understandably hazy, but I recall one rainy evening about dusk with the rain drizzling down onto a group of the 99th in some Algerian town. The town was inhabited by mental cases, one of whom was threating to beat in Bob Goad's head with a hammer. The man turned and seemed surprised to find me studying his shoulder blades. At any rate, he was content not to bash anybody's head in. Goad was killed four or five weeks later.

In case we were shot down and had to walk back from a mission we were given directions to go to Cape Spartivento (Sardinia, Italy) and show a flashlight. The pick-up boat could be expected to be a mite suspicious and to ask such questions as "Who is Betty Grable's husband?" Since I would have been utterly unable to answer questions about sports or movies, in order to keep from being mistaken for a squarehead (German)

I planned to declare myself an Arkie and to tell an Arkansas joke or two. Surely no Schutzstaffel clown would sink so low!

One of our chores was to regularly visit Messina, Italy to discourage the use of the ferries across the Straits of Messina. The place was heavily defended. While under aggressive fighter attack from the rear, I was busy shooting at ten o'clock, and every other gunner was also shooting, when a stray empty cartridge from the plane above came through the escape hatch on the other side of the forward hatchway. The cartridge case put a dent in my steel helmet, smashed my earphones, and sent me rolling on the empty cartridge cases which littered the floor. At first, I thought, from the sudden silence, that all four engines were shot out. The cold wind was tearing through the plane and dust was everywhere. But when I moved my head, I could hear a tinkle from the broken headset, I realized that I could feel the engines working away. I figured that I had time for one quick look before bailing out, so I crawled back into the nose and looked to the left, where two engines were spinning. That gave me time for a look to the right, where two more engines were churning away. Pete and I then went back to the political discussion.

It must have been in May 1943 that the Germans began head-on-attacks upon us. Since the B-17's, at that point, did not have nose guns, and the cheek guns could be used only on deflection shots, I was plumb mournful all the way back to Navarin. To my pleased surprise, as we came in on the approach I saw below on the hardstand three new B-17s with nose guns. We put them into the formation next day, and upon our return that day we found three more new planes with nose guns ready for the next mission, so we kept just a little ahead of the Krauts. This was accomplished through the system of Modification Centers, which allowed our assembly lines to continue while day-to-day intelligence was used to introduce modifications such as the nose guns.

Although delayed by the ferocious Mediterranean storms, when the skies cleared over Kasserine Pass the 99th Bomb Group was ready to drop leaflets on the tankers for which Rommel waited. We participated in the Cape Bon Massacre, as detailed in ROMMEL'S LAST STAND by Larry Cortesi.

We took out the torpedo factories, airplane factories, etc. The 99th led the first raid on Rome, where we blew up an ammunition train in the San Lorenzo yards. So much for so-called "open cities". I flew fifty missions in the supreme peace ship, the B-17 Flying Fortress. By the end of my tour I had to use both hands on the fork to get food into my mouth because my hands were shaking so badly. I weighed about 128 pounds and vomited much of my food back up after eating. Yes, I drank a lot.

Our ground echelon overtook us in May. We were pretty glad to see them, especially since this relieved us of many such duties as loading the bombs. It was good to have our own conscientious ground crew servicing the BTO. Among those who overtook us was an eager citations officer. After studying the reports of our raid on Milo and at Trapani, the citations officer is said to have written up a commendation for an individual bombardier who supposedly dropped a frag bomb onto the cockpit of a German fighter as it rolled down the runway for takeoff. This flight of fancy is supposed to have been returned with two appropriate words scrawled on it in Dolittle's handwriting.

French Intelligence warned us that a certain day in July had been selected by the local population for revolt. The Tauregs[10] had come in to pasture their camels on the barley stubble and since the Arab legion on Cape Bon, Tunisia had simply disappeared during the German surrender we were understandably suspicious of the whole situation. As the day drew near, I decided to give lessons. So, I set up a 600-yard range outside camp against the Djebel, (hill), using cardboard targets with only the X-ring blacked in. This could not be seen with the naked eye, but I was using my personal scope, a Weaver 440 mounted on a Springfield bolt-action rifle. The natives were interested. I enforced good range procedure, showing how many cartridges, I was about to load and keeping them behind the firing line. I snuggled down in prone position, looked into the mirage, and squeezed off my shots five at a time. The Arabs would then race me to the target, probably to make sure that I did not punch holes in by hand. In those days, I could put about half of my shots into the X-ring. The point of this hot, hard work was to convince the Arabs that when they came to castrate they should start over on the other side of camp. The appointed day came and went with a certain amount of gunfire, and maybe a few women shot, but no important killings. When you shoot into a Moslem crowd you don't hit men. The revolt was accomplished later, in 1948.

I find that I have a small collection of dogtags, acquired in the following manner;

Every six months the Army checks on the religious preference of each soldier. On each such count, I would change my religion, which would get me a new set of dogtags without my having to surrender the old ones.

The purpose of this skullduggery was to provide me with extra dogtags so that if I found myself the sole survivor of a crashed and burning aircraft out in the desert I might deposit a set of dogtags in the ashes while slinking away into the desert. The scuttlebutt was that if one could reach the Tauregs (no great problem), as a flier one would have a certain status and would be eligible for adoption into the tribe. The sheik would, supposedly, give one of his daughters to wife, and if a man could learn the language he might become sheik in time. Well, I never found a use for the extra dogtags, and when my tour was over I realized that I longed for western women rather than the human cattle which the harem is said to produce. Maybe those blue tattoos between the eyes had something to do with my decision.

---

10 The *Tuareg* people are a large Berber ethnic confederation. They principally inhabit the Sahara Desert, in a vast area stretching from far southwestern Libya to southern Algeria, Niger, Mali and Burkina Faso.

I tried to learn the language of the Setif[11] region from a shepherd friend, a young man who sold eggs and onions. In 1947 when I was a student at UNM I got an Arabic dictionary, but the words simply were not the same. In 1948 in reading Cunningham Grahame's books about Morocco I found a Shillah glossary, and there the words were. I had learned the lingua franca, Shillah. Arabic was spoken to about the same extent as Latin is in the US; it was spoken by educated churchmen. I kept it a secret from the Army because it would only hurt their feelings to be told.

Our area was plumb civilized. Although we had a slave market at Bou Saada, there had not been a coffle[12] sent up across the Sahara since 1933.

Figure 1: Tunisia
George F. Coen–1943

Our crew got to Algiers every six weeks or so. Since most of the girls seemed to have a child or two, we got to enjoy an hour or two of home life, just like big boys.

One day while giving my temperance lecture in the Navarin thirst parlor (liquor, down with it!) I heard a thunderous boom like a bomb dump blowing up. Stepping to the door, I took a bearing on the cloud and noted that it was in the direction of the 99th, about seven miles away. I re-entered the thirst parlor and got soused. Meanwhile the mighty Bombardier, P.G. Bulkeley, was helping to pick up the larger pieces for the mortuary squad. We lost about 16 men, and there were twisted bombs all over the ground adjacent to our tent. It seems that a new explosive had been introduced into our bombs, and the ordnance men had supposedly been warned to cease their old practice of simply jamming on the truck brakes while backing in order to unload bombs from the flatbed truck. There's always somebody who doesn't get the word.

---

11 **Sétif** Province is a province in north-eastern Algeria. Its capital and largest city is Sétif; the next largest city is El Eulma. There is also the World Heritage Site of Djémila there.
12 A group of animals or slaves fastened together in a line, or driven along together.

On one of our missions to Foggia, it must have been in July, we lifted off from Navarin and flew up to Hammam Lif to pick up the First Fighter. Although we circled their airfield, nobody came up to fly with us. The formation then went on course for Foggia, across the Mediterranean. It was pretty obvious, this being a penetration mission, that there would be enemy interception, so I worried. As we crossed the enemy coast, I spotted the First Fighter far below us, keeping up with us and steadily gaining altitude. Good old First Fighter! It was not long until they were at our altitude and riding out there at 1000 yards. Funny thing, though, their planes had swastikas on them. And the planes were Messerschmitts and Focke-Wulfs. So, our 100-plane escort did not relax me a bit. I squeezed off a burst or two at the head of one airplane driver, expecting to see the gang dive for cover when The Mighty Coen unleashed his wrath, but nobody paid any attention at all to me, so I saved my ammunition for the main event. The fighters then went up ahead and opened the ball. The Messerschmitts came in on the tail in waves of five and the Focke-Wulfs went wide to come in on the wings. All of the rear-firing guns were banging away when I noticed two FW-190s coming in at 9 O'clock level. The fire control cutoffs would prevent our turrets from shooting our own wing off, so the turrets could not shoot at these gents. I tried to bend my gun barrel to get the first plane, but it was just no use. About the time the first plane reached the 1000-yard mark the plane on our left dropped down, the plane on our right rose up, all three of the element dipped their left wings, and the turrets opened up. Stove-lids and stuff shredded off the Kraut and he lost interest in the game. His partner declined to come on in for his share, but dove without firing, so Buxton in the ball turret followed him down with a free shot. The top turret was about out of ammunition, so I gave Brad my reserve supply during a lull in the fighting which proved to be the end of that day's battle. The Germans went back to attack the next Group. Litwalk said that the rear-firing guns were getting one out of five of the ME-109s as they attacked from the rear. That is the only time I ever shot at a man's head. Well, almost only.

During April, May, and June of 1943 the German fighter pilots would break off their attacks as we entered the flak barrage and they would then immediately attack the following group of bombers. Since we would be out of breath and ammunition, we wondered why they did not simply stay with the group for an extended running battle. On the 5th of July, the Germans did follow one group for an extended battle, and that group was the 99th.

We were dropping fragmentation bombs on a complex of airfields on the planes around Gerbini, Sicily, and in the aerial battle with about 100 German fighters three of our planes were downed. Although I did not know it at the time, my buddie Sam Levine was one of the dead, due to a 20mm shell in his chest. I was not on the mission, but Imrie was. When he came into the tent after the raid he was a delicate shade of green and obviously exhausted.

Our plane led the group to the same target the next day. I took the group over to Gozo to pick up an escort of Spitfires, and we then proceeded with our loads of frags to Gerbini. A few ME-109s came up, but each dove for the deck with two or three spitfires on his tail. We bombed and went home. The Germans were by that time able to mount occasional full-scale attacks, but they could not maintain a full-scale offensive due to the pilots taking early retirement during the fracas. We were able to kill their irreplaceable pilots, and they were filling the ranks with green pilots. Their training program suffered from a shortage of gasoline, possibly connected to our visits to the cracking plants at Livorno and Bari Italy.

There was one vary hairy mission along about August. It was one of several to Foggia, Italy. Buxton and Swanson had been picked up by the MPs for clowning around in a sidewalk café and had been put on KP. We had Sammy Goodman for a replacement ball turret gunner.

Now our own crew was always very quiet and business-like during these group discussions with the Third Reich, so we were quite disconcerted to have Sammy conducting constant chatter over the intercom all the way to the target. All four officers later agreed that they had heard the same message from Sammy; that the waist gunners were hit and needed help. Sammy later refused to admit that he had said a word. At the time, the message came from Sammy, we were under constant attack, with all rear firing guns working away in fine shape.

Bob Imrie took the controls while Henderson made his way with a walk-around oxygen bottle through the open Bombay to aid the waist gunners. Henderson planned to replenish the little walkaround bottle at the fitting in the Bombay, not knowing that Imrie had removed it to replace a faulty fitting elsewhere. Somehow Henderson made the trip through the bombay anyhow, only to see nothing but asses and elbows and flying empty cartridge cases. Dub (Henderson) got back to his seat in time for the bomb run, and we completed our mission. It was no use saying anything to Sammy Goodman, we had too much respect for any ball-turret gunner to say much. But the insanity of breaking up a skilled combat crew on the eve of a penetration mission in the name of discipline remains with me yet. These gratuitous risks are hard on the nerves.

It was in August that on a routine visit to the BTO I discovered that the supply of morphine syrettes was not in place as it should be. I returned to the company area and reported the loss. I was told that when the loss was investigated, a further loss of morphine was found, along with a wet needle behind the copilot's seat. The investigation, if any, started with the Flight Surgeon's examination of us four officers in the nude, looking for needle marks. A few cactus needles were found in our hides, but no good evidence! This did not sweeten my temper a bit.

We also had trouble with looting of the bail-out rations, theft of sunglasses, etc. None of this was good for the nerves.

We were entitled to ten cents worth of candy per week, but since the PX was opened when the Group was absent on a mission, and since there was not enough to go around, we usually had to do without our Necco wafers and chewing gum. By the time I had 50 *missions, I had little matriotism and no patriotism worth looking for, and I feel that this country owes me about six packages of Necco Wafers from somebody's PX.*

English's crew, which had a tent next to ours, had a dog. I think that dog was a spaniel, and I distinctly remember that it was a male. My sack was always on the ground, for safety's sake and so that I might better hear what was going on around me. One day as I lay there in my sack on the ground the aforesaid dog came by and pissed in my face. It would have been wrong to yell at him; all that I could do was put a bullet into the ground near him and wonder how he knew that I was a Second Lieutenant. When English and his crew went down on their 50th mission the dog never missed them, he just took up with another crew.

Early on the fellows had started calling me Trigger, perhaps because I had my very own six-shooter on call. For whatever reason, when a firing squad was needed they would call me, and I would callously conduct an execution of the offender, leaving its eight legs but removing the body. At a distance of 3 feet this requires a bit of practice. Now (1988) I have reformed and am a friend of all spiders, no matter how large.

It must have been in July that we lost Hunter in Vicki. We had made a raid on Foggia from our base at Navarin, had come off the target and we were well on our way home when Hunter's #3 engine began to burn. Hunter had previously brought his plane home with an engine fire, and he attempted to do it again. The flames increased, while Punjab Imrie photographed the event, the flames burned through the main spar, it may be that the wrong engine was feathered. I watched in an insect-like series of movements; look at the plane, search for fighters, look at the clock. The whole sweep took about 20 or 30 seconds. When the fire burned through the main spar the wing came off, with its two engines still churning and turning. The plane then broke at the ball turret and flames wreathed the edges of the breached fuselage. The metal appeared to be burning. The left wing, with part of the fuselage attached, went on flying in a downward spiral with the two engines working. Considerable debris came out of the plane. The base boffins later billed the white debris as parachutes and the tail of the B-17 as a German fighter, in spite of our protestations that the supposed parachutes were just burning fuel cells, and that we were not under attack at the time.

Although it seemed at the time that nobody could have survived, Sgt. Titus did survive and escaped. He was killed a month or so later on another raid. And in 1986 another survivor checked in to the 99BGHS.

My most memorable mission was that of August 17, 1943 to Istres le Taube, France. On takeoff, the gas cap on one of our fuel tanks came off. The resulting stream of gasoline streaming past the engine exhaust was anything but reassuring, but there was nothing to be done at that time. We transferred fuel out of the offending tank and after a while the leakage ceased. This was the longest mission of our career, mounted from Oudna, near Tunis. About noon we raised the coast of France, passed the offshore islands, and went to discuss politics with the Krauts. The complex of airfields was loaded with aircraft all loaded with bombs and gassed for the purpose of attacking the allied invasion fleets moored at various ports for the invasion of Italy. We eased into the flak and dropped leaflets or something over the assembled planes. About 48 seconds after emptying the bombbays the German aircraft began to detonate, and as each craft blew up it triggered explosions to right and left, which triggered further fireworks. About that time, we observed pink flak, and about then we feathered one engine. The colored flak was a standard signal for the fighters to close as the flak ceased. I did not find this at all reassuring. In fact, I placed my feet as far apart as I could on the flight deck, and my knees still knocked together. We could not keep up with the formation but proceeded alone out over the ocean toward the closest port, Bougie, Tunisia. As we churned along alone a P-38 came abreast of us with one of his engines feathered. He was very gentlemanly, never pointing his nose at us, for Rossi had not been downed at that time.13 He then pulled in very slowly and carefully until he was tucked in beneath us, which made a nice little formation. I covered him with my machine gun until he was close enough for me to read the lettering on his parachute.

In this fashion we came, not to Bougie, but to the airfield at Bone. I believe that by then we had another engine feathered, and I was told that the red light had been on to indicate fuel shortage for five minutes. These lights were supposed to light up ten minutes before the tank would be empty. Henderson put the beast down, and we relaxed.

About an hour later the sky seemed to fill with B-17s. I first thought that we had received reinforcements, but I soon saw red flares to indicate wounded aboard. These proved to be the vanguard of the first shuttle-bombing mission. Three of them would line up with the little Bone runway, one would chicken out, and two would land. One promptly ran out of gas on the runway and had its tail sheared off by the next plane. The following plane removed another six inches from the stub of the rudder. I saw an Otter amphibian plane taxi in with more than one rescued aircrew clinging to it from planes which had ditched in the traffic pattern. Others landed in the dry lake. It was a gory mess. I went down to the seashore, removed the contents of my pockets and dove into the Mediterranean to wash the smell of fear off of me. By then I had forty missions and was quite ready to quit.

---

13 The story was of a crippled B-17 bomber coming back from a mission against the Island of Pantelleria. The crew was considering bailing out of their bomber when they spotted a P-38 coming closer. They immediately relaxed knowing it was coming to their aid. The crew continued to dump extra weight from the aircraft, including the guns and ammunition. Before the crew realized what happened, the P-38 erupted in gunfire and destroyed the B-17.
Several weeks before, a P-38 pilot was low on fuel and was lost. He actually made an emergency landing just outside of Sardinia. The pilot was captured before he was able to destroy his aircraft. Italian pilot, Lt. Guido Rossi came up with the idea of using this P-38 against the American bomber. Rossi's strategy was to wait until the bombers made their attacks. Rossi would then take off and scout around for stragglers. He actually used this technique to shoot down several bombers.

The Headquarters had counted my missions and arrived at 48 when my count was 49. Upon checking I found that Sam Dunn had credit for a raid on Sciacca. This did not bother me at all, because I planned to fly my fifty missions, say nothing about the count, and set up a small harem while awaiting exposure as a time-expired man. Alas, Sam flew a mission to Benevento and put my name down, so I had credit for 50.

When I had completed my tour of fifty missions the five gunners had only 48 to their credit. I had no desire to leave until they had finished their tour, for we had had several crews destroyed on their fiftieth raid. Now, although I had been clicking off several missions each week, all of a sudden, the pace slowed up, and it took two months for the crew to get two more missions. I had settled on a routine of staying drunk two days and then returning from my step brother's place at El Aouina, shaving, and collecting my mail. After one month of this routine I was pretty well worn out.

At that time, Terrible Terry Barton drafted me to fly with a group of pilots in a C-47 back toward the zone of the interior. (That's the land of the free, and a troopship back home). The weather was lowering, the pilots called me up front to navigate (using only the dashboard clock and my fingers). We iced up. We dropped down 500 feet. The ice broke off the wings). The ice reformed. We dropped down 500 feet. And so on, until we were well below the mountain tops there in the murk. However, we finally broke into clear over the Atlantic near Safi, turned south, and came into Casablanca for a landing.

The pilots did not wish to go to whatever base it was that served as staging area for the troopships, so we all went to the Air Base where the food was better. One of us had an ironclad deal with a friend up in HQ. This friend was to notify us when a troopship was in port and loading. Nothing could go wrong! So, we lay around the barracks doing nothing that I can recall, until one afternoon we got a rush call to get down to the docks. We got to the docks, and sat on our barracks bags on the pier, and watched troop after troop of soldiers board the big black ship. Darkness came. Troops continued to plod up the gangplank. Finally, the flow of troops stopped, and all got quite except for the flushing of ships toilets and an occasional mutter from one of us. After a very embarrassing half-hour somebody looked out of the ship and said to us "We think we have a place for you." We loaded on, and the stateroom was fine.

And so, we finally got a berth on the EMPRESS OF SCOTLAND (A confiscated Japanese liner). In view of a shortage of life rafts I visited the companionway leading to the Afrika Corps POW exercise area. A 50-caliber machine gun was mounted at the head of the steps. I asked the gunner what outfit he was from, and he replied "The 99th". About that time the Red Cross Man came over and informed me that the Geneva Convention forbade staring at the prisoners, so I went on, reassured.

The EMPRESS OF SCOTLAND zigzagged across the Atlantic alone and arrived eight days later at Newport News, VA. Our large contingent of Air Force men assembled on the docks, where no particular notice was taken of us. Presently one man went across the street to a phone booth. Presently another man, and yet another left the docks. Finally, some notice was taken – guards armed with submachine guns were posted around us to keep us in place. A young shave tail arrived and shouted, "Fall In". After several tries to get us into a military formation he resorted to pleading "Please Fall In, or we'll be here forever". We got into a column with the majors up front, and off we went toward Camp Patrick Henry.

As the column came up the road leading to the Camp, I could see from the rear, where we lieutenants were, that the fences were lined with men jeering the supposed new recruits who marched so badly. As the fighter pilots at the head of the column came abreast of the jeerers there was silence. We were the first combat men that this lot had seen. Camp Patrick Henry had no idea what to do with us, so we languished in the barracks. Finally, we sent a colonel over to the Air Base, and immediately an Air Force type showed up and placed us on orders for leave at our homes. My homeward trip took me to Indianapolis where I detrained for a few days at Ravenswood.

By now it was almost Christmas. I hitch-hiked on aircraft to Little Rock, thence via California to Salt Lake City for reassignment. I made my way from Salt Lake City to my next assignment, instructing second-phase navigators at Dalhart, Texas. That meant that the planes, which were B-17s, were flown by second phase pilots, men with about 6 weeks' experience in B-17s.

At Dalhart, I was placed on two sets of orders at the same time, one to B-29s which meant combat, one to pilot training. Had I been a captain I would not have been eligible for pilot training, but as it was I did get to pilot training.

In May of 1944 I was transferred to Amarillo because the Dalhart Base was being readied for closure.

In June, I went to Santa Anna as a pilot trainee. All of us officer trainees were sent through the Stanine Battery once again as controls. I was told by one of the testers that I had set a record for high score on the tests measuring devotion to duty. This pleased me greatly, especially when I went over the hill in July of that year.

In June, I went to Lake Tahoe, where I met Bettie. I was also able to visit her in her home at San Francisco.

I went to Dos Palos for flight training. I washed out rather promptly.

When I reported to the orderly room a bright young Second Lieutenant asked me how long I had been back from overseas, and when I told him he commented "oh, over six months." This scared me so much that I went to my quarters, packed a toothbrush, and headed for San Francisco without approved leave.

I proposed marriage to Bettie and made arrangements to get in touch with her wherever I might be sent next which ended up being Kirkland AFB, Albuquerque, New Mexico.

At Kirtland Field, I flew mostly in B-24s. Since the student pilots were Chinese, and I had no desire to add the language barrier to the other flying problems, I soon worked a deal with a Command Pilot (one with a star and wreath above his wings). I flew with him swinging compasses and with nobody else. By now I was so "shell shock" I could not have gone overseas a second time if I had wanted to.

By May 1945 the Air Force had begun to allow pilots to be discharged with as few as 19 points, merely 19 months of service. At Hobbs, where I was stationed, the opportunity for discharge occurred only on one Sunday morning with only 12 hours' notice. When I showed up at 0700 Monday the lists had been closed. Since I had 135 points I merely expected to get out in June of 1945, so I was not upset. By July or August there was a second call for navigators and bombardiers who wanted discharges, and the line was about two blocks long. This seemed to surprise the Air Force.

There were no discharges of navigators or bombardiers from Hobbs, although I believe that there were discharges at other bases. The point system seemed to have been forgotten. The original Sunday quota had caught the older men, married and living in town, by surprise. We lost Taylor about that time. He bailed out from straight and level flight, but his parachute failed. The parachute riggers were getting out.

By September 1945 my nerve was gone. I flew every three months, dosing myself heavily with sleeping pills. On my last flight, the left tire went flat. Leaving the B-17 wingtip about one foot above the runway on landing. That's when I quit flying, except of course that I would put my name on the Form One after a plane landed in order to get my flight pay.

When I joined the Armed Forces in April of 1940 we seemed destined to fight the Soviet Union along with the Axis, and I felt that I had very little chance of living out my three-score years and ten. I therefore became a dier, fatalistically awaiting the one with my name on it. When we arrived in Algeria there was no such thing as a definite combat tour, so it was reasonable to continue the assumption that it was all a one-way trip. However, the tour was set at 50 missions, so when I had 48 missions it was obvious that I might survive.

On the way, back from my 49th mission I sat on my ammunition box and for the first time, thought about this life which was being given back to me.

For the next twenty-five years, my father lived his life as a diagnosed, untreated victim of severe war trauma. There is no doubt that today his condition would qualify as PTSD.

2

COLLATERAL DAMAGE

My mother, Betty, was born on November 29, 1922, in Seattle, Washington. She had one younger sister, Helen. When Betty was 15, the family relocated to Redwood City, California, where she completed her high school education. During this time, her upbringing could only be described as wholesome and pampered. She enjoyed the best of what her parents had to offer.

In June of 1944, while on vacation with her parents at Lake Tahoe, she met George Coen. The afternoon prior to their meeting, she had been horseback riding and was thrown by the horse. Needless to say, she was the talk of the resort that evening. George had been asking about "That girl that got thrown from the horse". Someone pointed up to the balcony where she was standing, and I guess it was "love at first sight" for George.

As my mother tells it:

> *He was so handsome in his uniform with all those war ribbons. We got to spend a couple of days together, getting to know each other, before I had to leave, back to California with my parents. We began to correspond with each other by mail.*
>
> *Later that summer, George took the train up from Santa Ana, where he was stationed, and spent the weekend with me and my parents. We were very happy together.*
>
> *I received word from George that he was being transferred to Dos Palos, California, (Near Merced), for pilots training. A few weeks later, George called and asked if he could visit me at home. I, of course, said yes. When he arrived, he was very anxious. He told me that he had "washed out" of pilots training. He was expecting orders but had no idea where it would be. He was very concerned that he might be sent back into combat. We spent*

a day and took the train into San Francisco, toured around and enjoyed a perfect day. George told me that he did not know when we would meet again, but proposed that we get married as soon as he got to his next duty station, provided it was in the U.S.

I accepted. When I later informed my dad, he objected and tried to change my mind. That was an effort that he had learned long beforehand was futile. Yes, I was stubborn and determined. Secretly, I was looking forward to leaving home.

Figure 2:
George and Betty—1944

In August, George received orders to Kirkland Air Force Base, Albuquerque, New Mexico.

I was unaware that when George arrived at Kirkland, he was immediately sent to the "Flack Farm." The Air Force had become aware of his "behavior" which they labeled as "Combat Stress". He spent several weeks in the camp, which was located on the east slope of the Sandia Mountains. He spent his days turning wooden bowls on a lathe and learning basic photography.

By mid-September, George informed me that he had made arrangement for us to stay in married housing at the base and that I should plan on traveling to Albuquerque.

Much to my parents' dismay, I boarded the train and headed east. When I got to Albuquerque, George had arranged for me to stay with his friends, Dr. and Hazel Beebe. They had a small apartment that they rented to George.

I arrived in Albuquerque and settled in as we made wedding plans. We decided to be married in the chapel at Kirkland AFB, and then honeymoon in Santa Fe. Prior to the wedding we both had to be interviewed separately by the base chaplain. During my meeting, the chaplain sternly advised me that I should not marry George as he was showing "serious side effects" following his combat experiences. I could not be persuaded, perhaps it was the prospect of having to go home and face my father? We were married on September 24, 1944. I was 21 years old.

We had a wonderful honeymoon in Santa Fe, stayed at the La Fonda Hotel, went horseback riding and got to know each other.

Back in Albuquerque, George was training new navigators, which required him to fly in B-24's, not his favorite airplane.

In early 1945, George was transferred to Hobbs, New Mexico. He hitched a ride to Hobbs with another Air Force couple being transferred also to Hobbs. George wanted to find us a home before I came down and we moved our belongings.

George rented a little house with other service couples living as neighbors.

Hobbs was dry, dusty, and hot. When it rained, the streets turned into mud. The town itself was about two blocks long.

Finally, George got his notice to go to Tacoma, Washington, to be discharged from the Army Air Corps. (Tacoma was his station of enlistment; therefore, he was returned there for discharge.) What a happy day that was for us.

We took the train to Tacoma and stayed with Clara Van Sant, an elderly lady who was a librarian at the Tacoma Library. George met her when he was in Tacoma and was studying to take the test for Army Aviation Cadet School. She helped him find books to study to prepare.

When George was discharged, we went to Seattle and stayed with my grandmother Nana Potter. We were thinking that George would go to the University of Washington.

After going out to the campus and inquiring and putting up with the rain, we talked it over and decided to go back to Albuquerque and George would go to the University of New Mexico.

We took the train to Albuquerque and stayed with Hazel and Dr. Beebe and rented the same room we had before.

We bought a little house off 4th street on Hogs Head Ave. which has since been renamed Cherokee Ave. George enrolled at UNM to be a civil engineer.

George M. ("Tad") was born on June 28th, 1946, and Bettie Marie ("Bobbie") was born June 28th, 1947. In those days, they kept you in the hospital for two weeks after you had a baby. I was so weak when I got home from being in bed, so long. George had to hire help to clean and fix our meals.

In 1948, I took the train with Tad and Bobbie to Redwood City, California. I was planning on staying because George and I were having a few problems. I stayed with Dad and Mother and they were so glad to see their grandchildren.

I went back to work at Roos Brothers in Palo Alto, where I had worked before marrying George. Tad and Bobbie went to nursery while I worked.

After a couple of months of writing back and forth to George, he said he wanted me to come home because he missed me. After much coaxing and to the displeasure of my father, I packed up, and the kids and I took the train back to Albuquerque.

In 1949 George graduated from UNM with a Bachelor of Science in civil engineering. He went to work for the Bureau of Public Roads. As part of the Engineering Trainee Program, his first assignment was in Hot Springs, Arkansas.

While in Hot Springs, we visited George's father and step mother who owned the Coen Supper Club outside of Little Rock.

Sometime around 1950 George's engineering training program ended, and the constant moving began as he began project assignments. One of the first assignments was in Cloudcroft, New Mexico.

We were then sent to Grand Mesa, Colorado, and rented a cabin with a wood cooking stove. Talk about "new experiences," but I learned to cook on it and it was also our heat for the cabin. I would warm up bath water on the stove for Tad and Bobbie to give them a bath and then I jumped in and took a bath. I was not about to use the cold public showers.

Several years later, I read the book "No Life for A Lady" about a woman who was married to an engineer. Everything was very similar to my life.

From there we were sent to Glenwood, New Mexico. We stayed in a motel which was a pleasant change from cabin living. I loved it, it was so nice to live among the trees. In October 1951 Richard was born in Silver City, New Mexico.

My parents visited us in Glenwood and one afternoon we took them to the Cat Walk. Mother would not go across, but Dad did.

George's stepmother, Marie passed away during our time at Glenwood. He went back to Little Rock on the train for the funeral. In 1952, we were sent to White Rock, New Mexico, where Tad started the first grade. We were then sent to Granby, Colorado. Traveling was getting to be a bit much at this point with Tad having started school and Bobbie a year behind him.

In late 1952, we were sent to Mesa, Arizona, where Tad finished the first grade. Mother and Dad visited in Mesa. They were doing a lot of traveling before their move to Bainbridge Island, Washington.

My cousin Tom Potter was in the Air Force stationed briefly in Phoenix for training. He visited us for a weekend before he went overseas. He was a fighter pilot. Following graduation, he was sent to Korea. The sad news was he was shot down just a day before the Armistice was signed.

In 1953, we were sent to Payson, Arizona. In the summers, we lived at the Grand Canyon, where George was helping to rebuild the road to the South Rim. George hiked down to the river regularly. The trail was a burro trail, very narrow and steep. We enjoyed our stay there.

In Payson, during the school year, we rented a house, which was nice for a change. Tad went to the second grade and Bobbie started first grade.

One day when I was unloading groceries out of the car Tad decided to climb out of the car window to get out of the car. Tad fell and fractured his arm. We went to the doctor in Payson who set it and put a splint on it. He charged us $15, which George deducted from Tad's allowance at 15 cents a week for the next year or so.

In the middle of the night one-night, George heard gunshots from the town center of Payson. He got out of bed, dressed, and picked up his pistol, and left to go see what was going on. Three fellows had been drinking and were shooting out the streetlights. George shot in their direction, not knowing what was going on. George got in trouble by not minding his own business. Thanks to Dr. Cartmel, who helped get George out of his mess. George lost his job with the Bureau of Public Roads and was not popular in Payson.

The Payson incident was hard for me to handle, so in late 1953 we moved to Flagstaff, Arizona, and George got a job with a private engineering company. The change did us a lot of good and we really liked Flagstaff. Tad continued third grade and Bobbie went into second grade. Tad had Mrs. Bunch for a teacher and he will never forget her. She saw that he got his studying done and kept him interested in school as best she could. She picked on him and he started to do better in school. As for liking her, Tad could not wait to get out of her class and go on to the fourth grade. Bobbie went on to the third grade.

By 1955, Tad had his first summer job helping the milkman deliver milk for 50 cents a day. He got up at four-thirty in the morning to go meet the milkman for the deliveries. He was usually back by noon. Tad's next job was a newspaper route.

April 28, 1957 Patty was born in Flagstaff. Bobbie had a little sister to play with and she treated her like a little doll.

George's father, George E., and stepmother, Louise, moved to Flagstaff from Little Rock, Arkansas. They bought a mobile home and lived out in East Flagstaff where George E. got a job selling mobile homes. They had not been there long when lighting struck their mobile home and set it on fire. They were only able to save their little dog and some clothes that were so smoky they had to go to the cleaners. They stayed with us until they could get another mobile home.

George was home on weekends mostly, working out of town during the weekdays. His projects included laying out the town of Page, Arizona, where the Glen Canyon Dam was being built.

In March 1957, we moved to Santa Fe, New Mexico, when George got a job with a private engineering company.

George still had to work out of town a lot and would only be home on weekends. Tad finished the 6th grade at Manderfield school.

Tad did not have much money for himself depending only on a meager allowance that George was always confiscating from him for one thing or another. He could not please his dad if he tried. Tad took it and took it for a long while and finally he and his Dad got into it and George started to ease up on him. I could not interfere for a while and then I tried to talk to George about it. It helped some but not enough.

In August of 1960 our fifth child, Tom, was born in Santa Fe.

In 1962, when Tad and Bobbie were in high school, Richard in middle school, Patty in kindergarten, and Tom in diapers, I filed for a divorce. It had to be done. There had been too much conflict with the kids' dad over the past several years and we were getting to be an unhappy family.

For the first sixteen years of my life, I watched my father act out his anger by physically and mentally abusing my mother and me. His obsessive need to be alone in the woods and away from other people speaks to his difficulty with maintaining social relationships. His constant need to dominate and control, I believe, led to the eventual unraveling of his life in the early 1960s.

3

MY EARLY YEARS

I was born in Albuquerque, New Mexico on June 28, 1946. My sister, Bobbie, was born exactly one year later on June 28, 1947. At the time, Dad was a student at the University of New Mexico. He was studying engineering on the G.I. Bill, having recently been released from the Army Air Corps.

Over the next 14 years, I would be joined by three additional siblings: Richard (1951), Patricia (1957), and Tom (1960), My parents would divorce in 1962.

Formative Events

My earliest memories start about 1949 when I was 3 years old. By age four, I was old enough to remember hardship and abuse, particularly toward my mother.

From Albuquerque, Dad packed up the Pontiac and we headed east for the start of his engineer training program. I believe Dad had to report to Washington D.C. for orientation. It was on this trip that I have my first memory of my father being physically abusive to my mother. We were driving along; as usual, dad had the driver's side window down, with his arm resting on the door. Dad and mom where having an argument about something. Mom had a collection of several round silver bracelets from her grandmother that she liked to wear and when she shook her hand they jingled. As I recall, as the argument progressed, she was pointing her finger at dad and the bracelets were jingling. Dad reached over and stripped the bracelets off her arm and threw them out the car window. He immediately pulled over to the side of the road, and I recall the two of them searching the roadside for quite a while trying to find the bracelets. I believe they found two, but the others were lost forever. Mom was heartbroken.

By 1950 Dad's training program took him to Cloudcroft, in the mountains east of Alamogordo, New Mexico. Our house wasn't very much—they never were very much in the early days of our lives. No refrigerator; instead there was an ice cooler that stuck out the window. Mom shopped for groceries one day at a time. Mice in the house were a fact of life. Occasionally the windows had screens on them. Tin can lids covered up the holes in the wooden plank floor.

We would move about every 6 months. In 1951, I recall the winter in Grand Mesa, Colorado. Dad was working on a road project. The winter was very cold and snowy, and we were running out of food, but we couldn't get down to town to a grocery store. In desperation, Dad took his pistol and went out and shot a grouse. He was very concerned how he could explain that to me, and how I might explain it to the game warden who lived next door.

From Grand Mesa we went to Glenwood, New Mexico. In preparation for Thanksgiving, Mom bought a turkey; the only problem was, it was a live turkey. She pointed out to Dad in which barnyard the turkey was, and it was up to him to claim the bird. A couple days later, late in the evening, Bobbie and I accompanied Dad down to claim the turkey, him with his .38 colt revolver in hand and me with my sister in tow. Bobbie and I were told to wait outside by the appointed wall while he went inside the barn. We heard a gunshot, and he came out with the turkey hanging by its feet. We proceeded home to pluck and dress the turkey.

During that same time period, a neighbor friend killed a bear. We went up to see it. The man asked us if we liked bear meat. Dad said he had never had it before, so the friend chopped off a front quarter and handed it to Dad, bear claws and all. Dad took the bear claws down to the stream and left them soaking to get the flesh off of them.

In October 1951, my brother Richard was born. It was about this time that the "standard rules of punishment" were adopted and implemented: open palm swats to the rump, from one to three in number depending on the offense.

At Christmas that year, Mom's parents, Mel and Helen, came to see the new baby and celebrate Christmas. They stayed in a motel room next door. Following the traditional opening of presents we sat down for a lavish Christmas dinner of turkey (store bought) and all the trimmings. Sometime during the celebration, I committed some transgression. Dad announced the sentence ("one swat"), and the punishment was administered on the spot. Helen was furious! How could my Dad do such a thing at the Christmas dinner table? That evening, Mel and Helen retreated to their room. The next morning Mel appeared and announced that Helen was packing and demanding to go back to California. My getting a swat the previous evening had sent her over the edge. For the next twelve years of my parents' marriage, "Grandma Helen" had no tolerance for my father. And so ended Christmas 1951.

To the best of my recollection, I cannot remember my sister Bobbie ever receiving a swat. She was either better behaved, or the judgement standards were different? Not to worry: over the years I received more than my fair share.

From Glenwood we moved to White Rock, adjacent to the town of Los Alamos, New Mexico. As we left Glenwood and had traveled about 100 miles, I remember Dad asking my mother, "You did bring the bear claws up from the stream, didn't you?" She hadn't, which meant that he had lost his prized bear claws forever. It was about then that we began to experience my father's wrath towards my mother; in those types of situations, he was unforgiving, explosive, and on occasion, physical.

I started first grade in White Rock and was there about six weeks before we moved to Granby, Colorado. I was now 6 years old in late 1952. Dad was working on the road up to Berthoud Pass. I remember it being so cold there that on Thanksgiving Day, when a neighbor came into our house, the change from the cold to the warm shattered her glasses. It was 20 degrees below zero, and that was enough for Dad, as I recall. He bought a small utility trailer to pull behind the car, and we were headed for warmer country: Mesa, Arizona.

We spent Christmas of 1952 in Mesa. I finished 1st grade in Mesa, Arizona. From New Mexico, to Colorado, to Arizona meant three schools for the 1st grade.

While living in Mesa, the Korean War had started, and Dad was very concerned. He was still a commissioned officer in the Army Air Corps and was afraid that he might be recalled to active duty to go to Korea. He resigned his commission, something he was very proud of as he felt he had cheated the government out of one more thing.

We lived east of Mesa in a little place called Three Knolls, on the highway to Apache Junction. In the early 1950s, Arizona was still pretty wild, and carjacking and kidnapping were facts of life. This was during the days of the Lindbergh kidnapping, which was on every parent's mind. My sister and I would have to wait on the public highway to catch the school bus. Dad was always concerned about our exposure getting to and from the bus stop as well as waiting on the highway for the bus. Dad carefully surveyed the situation and then trained us on how we were to approach the bus stop with maximum caution. In order to cross the highway to wait for the school bus we would go through a concrete culvert underneath the road. Dad told me it was my job to walk through the culvert first, while my sister waited. I was to make sure that there were no potential kidnappers lurking at the other end of the culvert, and it was my job to give the all-clear. My sister would then come through the culvert and we would wait for the bus.

Dad spent a lot of time impressing upon me what my responsibilities were as the oldest. I was expected to take charge and care for my sister and my mother when he wasn't around. Dad was working on the road construction from Sunflower to Payson and lived in a road camp, coming home on weekends.

Black-and-white television had just been invented. I remember seeing Eisenhower on the television, but it was always at a relative's or friend's house as Dad didn't believe in television. During our time in Mesa we got to meet our cousin Tom Potter. Tom was an Air Force F-86 pilot and was stationed for a brief period at Luke Air Force Base, west of Phoenix. He came out several times to visit Mom and Dad. He then shipped out for Korea. He told Dad that he didn't expect to return.

In 1953, when I was 7, we moved to Payson, Arizona, and I started the 2nd grade. Dad was working on the highway construction from Payson to Mesa during the winter and from Williams to Grand Canyon City during the summer. About six months after our arrival in Payson we learned that cousin Tom Potter was reported missing in action in Korea and presumed dead. They had not recovered his plane or his body, and there was no further comment. Subsequently, in 2006, his remains were recovered and returned for burial at Arlington National Cemetery.

I remember our time in Payson very fondly. At times, Dad could be very kind and caring, not only to Mom but to us kids, and we had some very fun times in Payson. Every Sunday Dad would insist on going on some kind of picnic, and we would get out into the woods and have plenty of time for exploration. However, during this time Dad also became more physically abusive to my mom. Their arguments often resulted in violence on the part of my father. I recall one especially unpleasant situation where my father wrestled my mother to the floor, and as she was on all fours on the floor he rode her like a horse, laughing as Bobbie, Richard, and I looked on.

Dad was quite a pistol "crank," (a habit I guess he acquired from North Africa during the war). At this point, there was a fair amount of fear that some type of national disaster was going to occur, and people needed to be prepared. Korea had ended, and the Cold War was just beginning. Dad started storing up pistol ammunition by the case, and we also had a box where he stored emergency food rations. He kept emphasizing the need for self-preparedness. He began to teach my mother and me how to use a pistol. We would go out east of town to the pistol range that he had made in an old gravel "borrow" pit. We'd go out on Saturdays for pistol practice. He was especially keen on Mom knowing how to shoot because he insisted that she sleep with a pistol in bed with her when she was home alone. He became very obsessed with his pistol and had a left-hand holster made, which he would strap to the steering wheel of the car. He taught himself to shoot left-handed outside the window of the car. He was very concerned about how he would defend the family in case of an attempted car hijacking. He had a special load of bullets in his pistol. The sequence was, as I recall, two armor piercing bullets (to stop an oncoming car), two wad cutters (to immobilize the driver), followed by two general purpose (to finish off any witnesses). He was continually preparing himself for any kind of potentially violent event.

Figure 3: My first pistol shot

During the summers at the South Rim of the Grand Canyon, we lived in a one-room shack. Mom cooked on a Coleman stove. There was no refrigerator, no bathroom or plumbing; just the public bath house. Despite the hardships, summers at the Grand Canyon were magic. Dad converted the little two-wheel canvas-topped trailer (that he bought when we moved from Granby) into a place for Bobbie and me to sleep. It was just like camping except it was dry, mostly. Dad, Mom, and Richard would sleep in the shack.

I had a lot of Indian friends at this point in my life, Navajo and Hopi. I spent a lot of time just running free, like Tom Sawyer, in the woods around the south rim of the Grand Canyon with my Indian buddies. I remember getting into all kinds of mischief at the rodeo grandstands and other places we weren't supposed to play. I remember climbing up on top of the roof of the grandstands and getting caught by the sheriff and getting taken home to my parents. This was just one example of some of the mischief a 7-year-old boy can get into in such wonderful surroundings.

On Memorial Day weekend 1954, the peace of Payson was temporarily shattered by the "infamous" Payson gun fight. Payson, in those days, was a town very much out of the old west as described by the "Ox-Bow incident." A hitching rail still existed in front of the grocery store. The volunteer fire department was "any able-bodied person" who was capable of responding to the community fire alarm. If a fire or incident occurred that required civic involvement, the alarm was sounded by someone driving down Main Street honking the horn three times or firing three shots in the air with a firearm. This was the signal for folks to assemble and deal with a fire or whatever the problem was.

I was 8 years old at the time. We had just returned from a camping trip, unpacked, and gone to bed for the evening. When I awoke the next morning, I went into the living room and there stood my father in very bad shape. His face looked like somebody had taken a cast-iron skillet to his head and face. He had two huge black eyes and his face looked flat. He was obviously very concerned and there was obviously something going on, so he asked us to sit down and he said he would tell us the story one time and one time only. The story he relayed to us was this:

In the middle of the night he heard three shots coming from Main Street. He thought he smelled smoke, so he had got up, got dressed, and ran down to the grocery store where he thought the shots were coming from. This was about two blocks away from our house. When he got there, there was a man named Ralph Garrels sitting underneath the only street light in town, trying to shoot it out. He was obviously drunk. Words were exchanged, which led to Dad's reply, "If it's a fight you want, it's a fight you'll get." He returned to the house and strapped on his .38 revolver in his shoulder holster and a .22 revolver on his hip. He then returned to Main Street. At this point, the gentleman who started the ruckus had assembled two Navy sailors, on leave from Korea, and a girlfriend. As soon as they saw Dad, they immediately grabbed him and pulled the pistol off of his waist. The sailors proceeded to beat Dad as Garrels kept yelling for them to "hit him again." Somehow Dad was able to get his hand on his .38 and he shot in the direction of the voice and hit Garrels. At this point, all the attention turned to Garrels. They let Dad go and he ran toward home. He hid in the bushes behind the house, waiting there until daylight.

So that was the story as it was relayed to us that morning. I recall there was a newspaper article of the event sitting on the coffee table that morning with headline "Payson Whoop-De-Doo Jails 1, Hurts 1." I was old enough to read so I was reading the story out loud to my sister, Bobbie. Dad overheard me, and I was banished to my room. The paper disappeared. After 64 years I've finally found that *Arizona Republic* newspaper article.

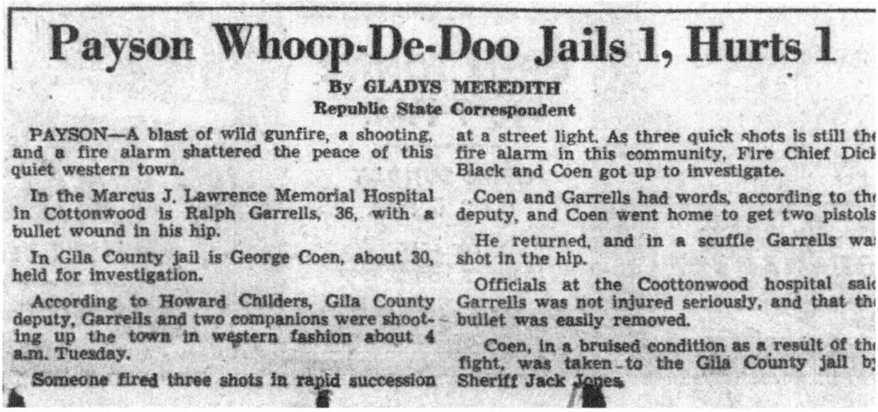

Payson Whoop-De-Doo Jails 1, Hurts 1

By GLADYS MEREDITH
Republic State Correspondent

PAYSON—A blast of wild gunfire, a shooting, and a fire alarm shattered the peace of this quiet western town.

In the Marcus J. Lawrence Memorial Hospital in Cottonwood is Ralph Garrells, 36, with a bullet wound in his hip.

In Gila County jail is George Coen, about 30, held for investigation.

According to Howard Childers, Gila County deputy, Garrells and two companions were shooting up the town in western fashion about 4 a.m. Tuesday.

Someone fired three shots in rapid succession at a street light. As three quick shots is still the fire alarm in this community, Fire Chief Dick Black and Coen got up to investigate.

Coen and Garrells had words, according to the deputy, and Coen went home to get two pistols.

He returned, and in a scuffle Garrells was shot in the hip.

Officials at the Coottonwood hospital said Garrells was not injured seriously, and that the bullet was easily removed.

Coen, in a bruised condition as a result of the fight, was taken to the Gila County jail by Sheriff Jack Jones.

Figure 4: The lost newspaper clipping

We were scared and had no idea what to expect next. Later in the day, the Pima County sheriff came up from Globe. He came to the house, heard the story, and placed Dad under arrest. Dad was asked to surrender his pistols, and he and the sheriff left for Globe and the county jail. The result of the whole event was that Dad was taken to jail in Globe, Arizona, where he spent 3 days. Although there is no public record of the arraignment, it appears that Dad was released for time served and had to surrender his pistols for 30 days. That was the sum total of his punishment. Some 20 years later, when I was in California, I ran into a gentleman from Payson who was a cousin of Ralph Garrels. He added to the story that Dad had shot Ralph in the hip and they had to take him to the nearest hospital which was in Cottonwood, Arizona, sixty miles away. We had a good laugh over it and he told the story the same as I remembered it.

This was also the year in Payson when I was trying to teach my sister how to climb in and out of the back window of the car. She was watching attentively as I showed her all the tricks when I inadvertently fell out of the car and broke my wrist. Mom took us to see the only doctor in town, Dr. Carpmell. He was a one-man show; any ailment, whether it was abortions or broken arms, he was capable of taking care of it. However, you first had to go get him out of the Ox Bow saloon. He sat down beside me and examined my arm. Yep, it was broken. He then took a couple of wood splints and heated them up in the kettle of water, so he could form them to my arm. He then, very skillfully, took my arm in his hand and popped it into place. He then wrapped my arm in the two wooden splints. He charged my father $15 to reset my arm. Back in those days my father was trying to teach us fiscal responsibility, and so we were paid allowance by check. Allowance was paid every week and the "check" was written on the back of his business card. Generally, the amount was between 5 cents and 15 cents per week depending on our age. We would then sign over the check to Dad in exchange for cash. It taught us the function of checks. I made 15 cents a week and I was required to pay back that $15 doctor bill to reset my arm. It took over a year to pay it off.

I started the 3rd grade in Payson, however, it wasn't to last. The Bureau of Public Roads, Payson District, was not impressed with my father's extracurricular activities. He was asked to leave the Bureau of Public Roads and to leave Payson, Arizona. Dad complied, left government service, and went to work for a consulting engineering company in Flagstaff, Arizona. Most of the time while we lived in Flagstaff, Dad worked out of town during the week and was home on weekends. This meant that Mom was without a car during the week. She would ride with friends to go grocery shopping or she would have to do it on the weekend when Dad got back.

A lot of things were happening during this period. Mel and Helen, my mother's parents, were very concerned about my mom and the treatment she was getting from my father. Mel was very unhappy with the life my father was subjecting my mother to. I believe Mel really felt that my mother had done the wrong thing by marrying my father, leaving him twice, and then going back to him in 1948. Mel and Helen would come for a visit once a year, and it was a time that we three kids always anticipated and enjoyed. Mel and Helen would pamper Mom and us kids. They would treat us to things we normally wouldn't get in our normal day-to-day life.

The first time they came to see us in Flagstaff, Mom and Dad and all of us kids were sleeping on the floor in bedrolls. None of us had beds at this point. Mom and Dad had a double bedroll in one room, and Bobbie, Richard, and I slept in bedrolls on the bare floor in another room.

When Mel and Helen came they would always stay in a motel. Mel always took very good care of Helen and always pampered her. Helen had an extremely good life, and Mel always thought that was the life that my mother was entitled to and would never see with my father. When Mel saw how we were living, he immediately went out and bought a bed for Mom and Dad. Shortly thereafter, a set of bunkbeds showed up by truck from Sears and Roebuck. Mel had ordered them and sent them to us.

I was in the 3rd grade when I got my first job. I would get up at 4:30 in the morning and walk in the dark to meet the local milkman. He would drive the truck around the neighborhoods delivering milk. I would run from the truck to the customer's front door with the glass milk bottles. I would run back with any empty bottles left on the porch. We would usually finish up around noon and he would give me 50 cents for the morning's work.

From the 4th through the 5th grades I had a paper route, during which time Mel visited us. Mel was in the newspaper business, so he quickly ascertained that I wasn't much of a businessman. I had been collecting for papers from my customers 2 and 3 months in advance to pay for my current month's paper bill. Long story short, I was indebted to the newspaper company because I had been spending money on bubblegum instead of paying the paper-company bill. Mel sat me down, set up a set of cash receipts ledgers and got me on a firm business basis. After a firm scolding he bailed me out with the paper company. I promised to follow the straight and narrow in the future.

Mel also saw that Bobbie and I were past the roller-skate phase and were now in the bicycle phase. There was no way our parents could afford bicycles; Dad just didn't make that kind of money. One day, following a recent visit, two beautiful 3-speed racing bikes showed up from the Sears and Roebuck catalog. Mel had ordered them for us so that we would have bikes like all the rest of the kids. Unfortunately, they were the new "skinny-tire" bike, not well suited for the roads in our neighborhood. All our streets were dirt with lots of stickers, so flats were a big issue. Dad made a bit of a joke about it. Dad never felt that Mel had much practical experience and certainly didn't exhibit it in this purchase. I also believe he resented Mel and Helen's intervention, feeling threatened by them.

We did a lot of camping in those days. When camping we always slept on the ground without a tent. Cooking was done over an open fire. These trips meant a lot of work for my mother. We'd come home with a box of dirty clothes and lots of dirty dishes. Dad would hop in the car and go off to wherever he was working that particular week and we would be left to clean up the mess.

About this time, we got a telephone. To use the early phones, you'd pick up the receiver and give the operator the number that you wanted to be connected to. We didn't have a dial telephone yet.

Toward the end of 1956, Dad and Mom announced that we were going to have a new brother or sister. Whenever my mother was pregnant, there was lots of anticipation and Dad would treat Mom differently. Her pregnancy with Patty was no different. He was tender with her, catering to her like a queen. Maybe that's why she ended up having five kids, because those were times she could look forward to some very special treatment. I recall that when Mom was pregnant she always looked special. Memories of Flagstaff include every Sunday going out on a family picnic. Lunch would be packed, usually hot dogs, fried chicken, or a picnic ham. Popular destinations included Sunset Crater, Mormon Lake, Oak Creek Canyon, or just the national forest.

One particular summer Sunday we went down to Oak Creek Canyon. It was warm enough to wade in the creek; I didn't know how to swim at this point. After lunch, I wandered off by myself. While wading downstream I stepped into a deep hole that was well over my head and I was in definite danger of drowning. As I went down for the 3rd time I recall looking up, and the last thing I saw was someone diving into the stream coming towards me.

A stranger did reach me and was able to pull me out and handed me to somebody on the bank. I was dazed and groggy, still not aware how close I'd come to drowning. I just wandered off back to camp with no realization of the significance of the event that had just occurred. A few minutes later, at the picnic spot, a lady came up and told my Dad, "Do you realize that your son just almost drowned". She proceeded to tell my parents about the incident. She explained how a man had dived in to save me and cracked his head open on a rock. They were now in the process of taking him to the hospital? So, we bundled up and went to the Sedona Hospital to see how the man was doing and, as I recall, Dad paid his hospital bill. It was about $50 . I recall there was some discussion as to how I would be required to work to pay it off. For some reason that never became a reality. I guess the fact that I had almost lost my life was considered restitution enough. Nothing was ever said other than the fact that I was talked to very sternly about the dangers of walking downstream. You always walk upstream so if you fall into a hole it will sweep you back out. Swimming lessons became a priority.

About this time, Dad went to work for the U.S. Forest Service. As a civil engineer, he helped design and build many of the logging roads around the Coconino National Forest. Working for the forest service meant that at any time he could be called upon to help fight forest fires. His job was firefighter first and an engineer second. Dad eventually left the forest service. He had problems with jobs and personalities and it seemed like there was always somebody he was struggling with.

Dad went to work for a consulting firm on a project in Tucson, Arizona. The family stayed in Flagstaff, and he would leave on Sunday night and drive to Tucson. He would return on Friday nights. Mom and us kids began to enjoy that way of life. There was a lot less tension when Dad was not at home. I was in the 5th grade and beginning to spread my wings. Dad had some pretty definite ideas of what I should be doing in the way of responsibility and work while he was away. He and I began to butt heads a little more at this stage. I began hanging out with kids who had a lot more freedom than I was used to. I was definitely pushing the limits and headed for trouble.

Upon completion of the project in Tucson, Dad was transferred to help establish the new town of Page, Arizona. The new Glen Canyon Dam was under construction. As a civil engineer, Dad was responsible for surveying and laying out the streets and utilities for the town of Page. I was starting the 6th grade. Bobbie was in the 5th grade. My 6th-grade teacher was Mr. Voorhees, who supported the "free spirit" concept and encouraged experimentation. That included school attendance. Since I was well along on testing boundaries, I took him at his word and ditched my first day of school. I recall that when I got home that night my sister had already told my mother that I hadn't been in school that day. The next morning, Mom hopped on my sister's bicycle, because Dad had the family car up at Page, and rode up to school. She then proceeded to give my teacher and the school principal a thorough tongue-lashing. She was very upset at not being informed of my absence from school the previous day. That ended the teacher's permissive attitude towards truancy. I also got paddled by the principal.

By this time, besides truancy, I'd become an accomplished dime-store thief. Not having any spending money, I took to lifting yo-yos and the like. I was definitely headed for a life of crime in Flagstaff.

The absence of my father during the week took a lot of pressure off of the family, and when he was there, the time that we spent together as a family was quality time. Dad was beginning to mellow out, although he still had fits of rage. It was not uncommon for him to heave a coffee cup at my mother occasionally. She never had a full set of dishes because Dad was quite a plate thrower. If something didn't quite fit him, he wasn't against tossing a saucer or breaking a chair. He had a very uncontrollable temper at this point in his life.

The Big Move to Santa Fe, New Mexico

In 1957, I was 11-years-old, the Edsel was the car of the day, and it was announced that we were going to move once again. Dad had decided to relocate the family to Santa Fe, New Mexico, as he had secured a job with an engineering firm in Santa Fe. He left first and began commuting every week. He found a house to rent and began the process of moving the family. We still had the two-wheel trailer, so he would take a load over every week. After about six weeks the last move was all of us—Bobbie, Richard, Patty, and me.

After arriving in Santa Fe, Bobbie and I were absolutely convinced that we had moved to a foreign country. The culture shock moving from Flagstaff to Santa Fe was severe. We did not like Santa Fe. The strong Catholic, Spanish influence in Santa Fe was totally foreign to us. We didn't live where most of the other "gringo" kids lived, so we felt like foreigners.

One of the most brutal parts, for me, in the move to Santa Fe was finishing out of the sixth grade in Manderfield School with Ms. Baca. In those days, Ms. Baca was a legend. She was an old maid, never been married, and a staunch Catholic. Each morning we stood facing the flag and recited the pledge of allegiance. We would then turn 90 degrees and face the crucifix and a picture of Christ hanging on the wall, adjacent to the American flag. We would then spend three minutes in prayer. Things that you would never get away with today. She had a code of honor system and everybody worked for merits and demerits. Class was regimented, and Ms. Baca was very set in her ways. After school on Mondays, she would line up all the Catholic students and march them over to Christo Rey Church, next door, for catechism.

If you made it through Ms. Baca's class, you had been someplace. It was totally foreign to me, and I had a very difficult time adjusting to it. To add insult to injury, she was convinced that I was undereducated, and so at the end of the sixth-grade school year she remanded me to summer school, which I was deeply distressed over. She would pass me on to the seventh grade only if I would agree to go to summer school. In my mind, I wasted my first summer vacation in Santa Fe going to summer school. Somehow, I got through summer school and memories of Flagstaff began to fade.

Our house in Santa Fe was a large old adobe. We initially rented the house, but later Dad was able to buy it. This was the first house that we ever owned. With the purchase of the house, it seemed that Dad became much more obsessed with money and making sure any employment uncertainty wouldn't threaten the ability to pay the mortgage. Purchase of the house was a family decision, and we were all made aware that home ownership included appropriate responsibility and sacrifice. House maintenance and repairs became a joint effort.

Mom ran her part with frugality and dedication. Three square meals a day. Breakfast for my father was two fried eggs, basted, sunny side up, two pieces of bacon, hot cocoa, toast or oat cake. Mother joined him at the table with one egg and coffee. While Dad had his breakfast, Bobbie and I were in the kitchen fixing our lunches. Our breakfast was usually hot cereal, corn meal mush, cracked wheat, or grits. Occasionally we got French toast or crepes. Never eggs or dry cereal. Dinners were always well planned and balanced. Pinto beans and something with hamburger were the staple. Never steak or pork chops. Occasionally a picnic ham or pot roast.

In 1958, I attended Harvey Jr. High School for the 7th grade. I got to add an elective class, wood shop, much to the disappointment of my father. Having the freedom to leave campus at lunch and move about the building between classes was empowering.

Report cards took on a new significance as grades were much more specific as to class content. Dad had very high expectations for me when it came to performance in the math, english, and science curriculum. His approach to extracting high performance from me was restriction versus reward. Extracurricular activities, anything not related to "studies," was to be earned by high scholastic performance. I was a C student; he wanted A's. The result was that my participation in after-school activities such as sports, dances, and football games, was not permitted. In my father's eyes, I just needed to study harder.

The tension between my father and me began to build as I resisted his attempts to dominate me. During the summer, I got a job with a neighbor, Captain Newsom, a retired Navy captain. He had a large house about a half mile up Cerro Gordo Road from our house. He paid me 50 cents an hour, by check. The job was great. I was becoming independent and learning lots of new skills, like weeding, lawn mowing, raking alfalfa, and cleaning the swimming pool. To ensure that I didn't squander my new-found wealth on frivolity, Dad decided that it was time that I began buying my own clothes. I have been doing that since I was 13 years old.

In 1959, I began the 8th grade, again at Harvey Jr. High. Dad required me to select classes that favored a college preparatory curriculum—no art or shop, just spanish and science. My grades did not improve, which also meant that my socialization skills had little opportunity for development. Friction continued to develop between Mom and Dad. In response to my lack of academic achievement, Mom would meet with my teachers, who would try to assist. Dad was convinced that I was just lazy, and more restriction was the answer.

About the same time, for some reason, Dad put Mom on a strict allowance with which she was required to feed and clothe the three other children as well as being responsible for all household maintenance costs, including washing machine repairs.

Wednesday evenings were always a very tense time after dinner. Dad would retreat to his room to ritually "figure the budget." Mom would start scouring the Wednesday newspaper grocery ads looking for bargains and trying to plan the next week's meals and her Friday shopping list. Mom's "allowance" was somewhere around $15–$20 per week. If there had been any unusual expenses during the previous week, you could count on Dad deducting it from her allowance. So, we would anxiously await the budget verdict. Dad would step out of his room and thrust Mom's "allowance" out to her. She would shriek, "How am I going to feed you with this?" After much negotiation, sometimes Dad would relinquish an extra $5. Other times she would just return to the newspaper ads and try to figure next week's meals with four instead of three dinner meals of pinto beans.

Saturdays were spent working on the house repair list. Sometimes this involved going down to the lumber yard for supplies. Some Saturdays after a morning of chores, Dad would seem to be in "the mood." He would call the local delicatessen/liquor store and order some cheese and three quarts of Schlitz beer. Mom and Dad would enjoy a glass of beer and listen to the Metropolitan Opera on the radio. Depending on how the previous Wednesday night had gone, she would use these occasions to plead her "allowance" case. She would extract some short-term relief, which usually meant that an afternoon "nap" was in order.

I spent the second summer working for Capt. Newsom and was growing more independent and defiant by the day. Toward the end of 1959 we kids were told that we were going to have a new brother or sister. In August 1960, my brother Tom was born.

The fall of 1960, I started the 9th grade and my last year at Harvey Jr. High School. Things began to get rougher between me and my father. It was like a perpetual poker game: "I see your hand, raise you two." I was now openly defying my father. There was nothing left that he could take away from me, no additional detention possible. In defiance of my father but with my mother's support, I enrolled in driver's education as a school elective. I also managed to get on the high school wrestling practice team. I would practice with the varsity squad after school and then walk the four miles home in the dark. Dad was working out of town mostly, so I found little resistance. Not to be outdone, Dad decided it was time I paid room and board, 50 cents a week. As my room and board "account due" approached $10, Dad decided he would no longer ignore my insolence. I was no longer welcome at the dinner table and the evening meal was withheld. Recognizing the writing on the wall, I gave up the wrestling team and got an after-school job at the local corner grocery—after school Tuesday through Friday till 6:00 pm, all day Saturdays. I walked the 2 miles home after work in the dark. I was being paid 50 cents an hour, and I was now buying most of my own food as well as clothing. I complied with the room and board requirement, grudgingly.

Money was a continual issue between me and my father. By now he had very little influence in my academic pursuits. Dad and I continued to fight it out, and he began to apply pressure on Mom to discourage her loyalty and support for me. I surrounded myself with a couple friends at school but mostly kept to myself, my job, and just trying to survive with little thought of what would really happen to me after high school. It all seemed unreal and impossible.

Fall of 1961, I started Santa Fe High School in the 10th grade with a rigorous schedule of college prep classes and with no idea what college was or how I would get there. I found myself in arrears on room and board for some reason, probably because of my having to buy new school clothes and pay school fees.

In desperation, I resolved that I would no longer pay my hard-earned cash to my father while he continued to abuse my mother on the subject of money. Independent of my father, I decided I would contribute directly to the welfare of the house, or family, bypassing him. My first project was to correct a very problematic plumbing problem involving the kitchen sink. On my own I designed fittings to intercept the kitchen drain under the house by purchasing new plastic pipe, fittings, and rerouting the drain underneath the house to the septic tank.

On my school lunch hour, I bought the required pipe and fittings from the local Sears store. I arranged to pick the pipe up after school, which I did. After school, I walked the 2 miles to my corner grocery store job, with the pipe over my shoulder. After work, I walked home in the dark with the pipe and crawled under the house to set about my project.

I could hear the family at the dinner table above me. I knew Dad could hear me scuffling around, but he chose to ignore my presence. I had prearranged my task and had the needed tools hidden in the crawl space. After about 30 minutes, I had successfully completed my task. I then went inside to confront my father who was still at the dinner table. With the receipt for the material I had purchased, which exceeded the balance of my room and board arrears, I stated my case and asked to participate in the evening meal. He replied, "No there was more to it than that and we would have to resolve that first." I went to my room, once again convinced of the futility of getting along with my father. Later that evening my mother snuck me some food. The tension and resentment between my father and me was still at a high boil!

Several days or weeks later, the final flashpoint occurred. I was in the kitchen with my mother and sister, who was fixing her lunch. I don't recall that I was doing anything of note other than talking with the two of them. My father came storming out of his adjoining room, in a rage, and announced that I was not allowed in the kitchen; the kitchen was "women's work." He was puffed up with clenched fists demanding obedience. This was the last straw, I grabbed a wooden chair that was sitting nearby and proceeded to have at him. I don't recall much of what happened next. Mom was screaming, and Dad was trying to get at me. With the chair in pieces on the floor, I made a hasty retreat and headed for school.

The End of The Marriage

Late that evening, I walked home from work. Outside the house, huddled under the elm tree, was my mother puffing on a Salem cigarette. I had never seen her smoke before, although I knew she had smoked as a young woman. I asked her what was going on, to which she replied, "I did it, and I've thrown him out."

In 1962, Mom as her first act of liberation and last act of defiance, started smoking again, a "right" she coveted shamelessly for the rest of her life. After 17 years of marriage and 5 children, my mother had called it quits. Mom had gone down to the court and gotten a restraining order and filed for divorce. Sometime later we learned that Mel had been instrumental in helping her get through it all.

Mom served Dad with an eviction notice. Shocked and astonished, he proceeded to move into the adjoining apartment in the back of the house. He quickly set about trying to reverse the sudden turn of events. He summoned Mom over to the apartment to try and renegotiate things. He promised mother an increase in her allowance if she would just quit this divorce foolishness. She stood her ground, and in the subsequent divorce decree Dad was ordered off the property. Dad was ordered to pay child support, about $150 a month. Mom was left the house and the mortgage. Dad was granted child visitation, two hours each week, on Sunday afternoons. Visitation was to take place in Mom's house at 2:00 pm. Mom was to vacate, and all of us kids were to be present.

This situation was doomed from the start. Dad refused to pay the child support, saying he couldn't afford to maintain a separate residence for himself and pay child support at the same time. The visitation sessions were a joke; he would sit in one corner of the room and read a book, and we kids would sit in the other corner and glare.

Despite numerous admonishments by the divorce court, my dad continued to antagonize and attempt to control his estranged family. For several years following the divorce decree, he grudgingly accepted partial fiscal responsibility for child support by imposing mandatory visitation on my three youngest siblings.

After several months, mother's situation became desperate. She had a job selling retail, but with two young children requiring day care there was no way she could keep up with the bills, and Dad made no attempt to honor his responsibilities for child support. Mom kept falling further and further behind. She "borrowed" money from every relative she could, but it was a losing battle. Meantime, winter had set in, roof repairs became necessary, septic issues developed, and the situation was getting hopeless.

To the rescue, grandparents Mel and Helen showed up. Mel took one look at the situation and went to work. An attorney was hired, home repairs financed, and stability restored. Judge Scarborough convened a hearing to consider the issues of child support and visitation. As part of this hearing Bobbie and I were interviewed by the court regarding our feelings toward visitation. During this interview, I told the court that given the choice I would prefer that visitation not be mandatory or compulsory. At the hearing, Dad was ordered to begin making regular child support payments and to begin efforts to pay the amount in arrears in monthly installments. The judge then ordered that my dad was to have no further control of me. My mother was given sole custody. At the end of the session, Judge Scarborough told my father that if he ever saw him in his court room again, Dad was going to jail.

Through all of this turmoil, I somehow completed my sophomore year at Santa Fe High School. I spent the summer with my little "weeding" enterprise and finished the summer with Mom signing for my driver's license. We had two cars at the time of the divorce, a 1959 Ford station wagon and a 1953 Pontiac. Mom was left with the Pontiac, a solid and safe car but she decided she wanted something newer. A local garage talked her into trading straight across for a 1957 Plymouth, tail fins and all. Unfortunately, it was a piece of junk, but that's another story.

I started my junior year at SFHS in the fall of 1963. I had very high expectations: driver's license, no more academic restrictions, and a chance to try out for the football team. As it turned out, as a junior, I lacked basic football knowledge, physical fitness, and countless other required traits. I was cut in the second week. To supplement my income, I went back to work at the corner grocery after school and on weekends.

Mom was trying out a variety of income-producing opportunities. With two small children, one still in diapers, her options were limited. She sold Avon for a while, worked as a waitress at the Santa Fe Airport, and ultimately settled on retail. She developed a love for selling cosmetics and found a niche at the local Payless Drug store.

Money was very scarce. Dad was still doing the minimum requirement regarding child support. He was several thousand dollars in arrears with no attempt being made to get current. Quite frankly, I'm still not sure how Mom held it together. I learned some time later that she had to resort to pawning her wedding ring, so the kids would have milk. She fell into the trap of not making the monthly house mortgage payment. She refinanced the house to keep from losing it and used the cash to make some critical roof and septic repairs. She borrowed money wherever she could. My two uncles and grandfather did their best to keep her afloat. It wasn't long before she realized something had to change if she was going to survive.

Mom had a very strong network of friends that did everything they could to help. Somehow through a couple of these friends she found a family, the Roses, that were interested in trading houses. They had a small but nice three-bedroom house down in the "development" section of town, and they were interested in our "Old Adobe" up in the barrio of Cerro Gordo.

The deal was done, they paid off Mom's mortgage delinquency, and we packed our belongings and swapped houses. By this time, I had barely managed to get through my junior year at Santa Fe High School. I had developed the destructive habit of skipping classes and school altogether. Mom's 1957 Plymouth was in constant need of repair and I had developed an interest in auto repair, so I would just stay at home and work on the car. That proved to be an exercise in futility. Mom returned to the car dealer who had traded her out of the perfectly good Pontiac. She was able to get him to take the Plymouth back and he gave her a 1947 Chevrolet coupe.

Two Important Men

I started my senior year at SFHS by signing up to repeat a semester of chemistry. At registration, my chemistry teacher just smiled and said, "George, if you will just come to class you will do fine." I finished the semester with a B. With the absence of my father's usual disapproval, I signed up for my first high school vocational course, auto mechanics. This was a true turning point in my life. The auto mechanics teacher, Mr. Polo Sena, was a godsend for me. First, I devoured the course material and finally saw a vocation, auto mechanics. Second, he quickly caught on to my personal "broken home" situation. Within a few weeks he suggested that I go meet Jack Marsh, who was the local Shell service station owner. Jack offered me a job at the service station; self-serve was unheard of in those days. I worked after school and on weekends. I got to work around cars and learned how to service them.

Mr. Sena then went about becoming my best friend. He would invite me to accompany him fishing on Saturdays at least once a month. Years later, in retrospect, I am convinced that he was one of two people who saved my life as a teenager and gave me an example to look up to. By his example, he taught me what it looked like to be a man, husband, and father.

The second person was Santa Fe County Sheriff, Perez Roybal.

By now, I was trying to spend as little time as possible at home. Relations between Mom and my sister Bobbie were testy at best. My brother Richard was feeling his oats and trying to take charge. It was not unusual for me to be in arguments with one or both of them. Occasionally these arguments would turn physical. On one of these occasions I was having a disagreement with Bobbie and I ended up slapping her. I then left the house and retreated to my favorite hangout, Jack's Shell station. I could always go to work. Later that evening, Sheriff Roybal drove into the filling station and asked for me. Apparently either Bobbie or my Mom had called the sheriff regarding our dispute and my physical reaction. Sheriff Roybal had figured the situation out. Without fanfare, he just said, "Be in my office tomorrow after school at 3:00 o'clock."

For the next several months, Sheriff Roybal and I had a standing Wednesday meeting, his office at three o'clock. We would spend an hour together, just talking. How was I doing? What was I going to do when I graduated? What where my interests? That was the end of my troubles at home. Between Mr. Sena and Sheriff Roybal, I started on a road that lasted a lifetime. A road of responsibility, integrity, and honesty. From these two men, I learned how to dream and then reach out and make those dreams a reality.

Mr. Sena was every young man's role model. Besides being a strong family man of deep faith, he was an example of accomplishment. He lacked a college degree, but no matter, he was a fantastic vocational skills career teacher. As a young man, he had joined the Navy and served aboard a Navy destroyer. After leaving the Navy, he was recalled and served in Korea. Following the cessation of hostilities, he returned to Santa Fe and worked as an auto mechanic for the local Ford dealership. Each year when the New Mexico State Police got a new batch of cruisers, they would always call Mr. Sena to outfit the new cars with police equipment.

4

MY PREPARATION FOR WAR

While lounging around the school yard during lunch break, about midway through my senior year, the conversation developed among us guys as to what we were going to do following graduation. I had no clue. One guy said he was going to join the Army. I thought about that for several days, discussed it with Mr. Sena, and then announced that I was going to join the Navy.

Why Navy? That was the only branch of the military that didn't wear a necktie as part of the uniform.

I then began conversations with the local Navy recruiter. Fortunately, as it turned out, he was a man of honor and integrity. I told him that I just wanted to be a mechanic. He sent me down to Albuquerque for a physical and a whole battery of aptitude tests. He then came up with a plan.

With graduation scheduled for the end of May, I would still be 17. My 18th birthday was not until late June. I guess I must have done fairly well on the aptitude tests because the recruiter was trying to steer me in a different direction. First, he suggested that because I was just 17, I qualified for the "Kiddy Cruiser" program, which meant that my mother would have to sign to get me in, but the Navy would have to discharge me before my 21st birthday, a three-year enlistment. At the time, I didn't appreciate the significance of this approach. Second, he offered a program that my test scores qualified me for, whereby I would go to the Naval Academy at Annapolis. I wasn't sure about Annapolis, but I was willing to go along with whatever he suggested.

At that point in my life, joining the Navy was the best way to get away from home and out of Santa Fe. I didn't talk with the recruiter about Navy life; I was content to fashion my own vision of what Navy life would be like. I'd seen the recruiting posters with the sharp-looking sailor standing beside the tall sailing ship looking into the sunset. That was enough for me. I had visions of going to the Mediterranean and getting to know the olive-skinned girls. This must have been obvious to the recruiter because he was intent on creating a program for me that would take care of me whether I believed I needed it or not.

Graduation came and went. My picture was in the local newspaper, swearing my enlistment oath. To make all the numbers work, I was sworn into the Navy before graduating from high school. I then took six days leave to complete my graduation requirements.

I was told by my recruiter to pack a shaving kit only. I was to travel by train from Albuquerque to Chicago to attend the Great Lakes Naval training center, "Boot Camp."

I said my goodbyes, a short visit with my father who had bought me a shaving kit and small traveling bag for my journey. His parting advice, "Take care and watch out for the whores."

The appointed day arrived. Mom drove me to the bus station in Santa Fe, where I was supposed to get the bus for Albuquerque to meet the train. After waiting about ten minutes past the scheduled departure with no sign of a bus. Mom decided she needed to drive me to Albuquerque to make sure I didn't miss the train.

We had gotten about 10 miles out of town when I saw the Greyhound bus in the rear-view mirror. I got Mom to pull over and I flagged the bus to stop. As I left the car I recall my mother's final farewell: "I trust your father has discussed the birds and the bees with you" and "Don't come home with a tattoo."

I was on my way to who knows where, naïve and completely oblivious to what was going on in the world outside of Santa Fe, New Mexico!

Training and Preparation

When I started High School in 1961, I don't recall having any serious knowledge or understanding of Vietnam, either as a country or a conflict. My family was busy worrying about life after divorce, John F. Kennedy had been elected president of the United States and moved into the White House. What was lost on me was that with him came a vision of Vietnam as both a "proving ground for democracy in Asia" and a test of American responsibility and determination. As the Vietcong saw it, the civil war between the two Vietnams was a continuation of the struggle against French colonialism. They contended that they were fighting a revolutionary war of national liberation. In their view, the French had been replaced by "American imperialists".[14]

By the end of 1963, I was halfway through my senior year of high school, President Kennedy had been assassinated, and the newly sworn-in "President Johnson vowed to press forward with the policies of the Kennedy administration.

> *… and the number of American advisers in South Vietnam had jumped to more than 16,000. Americans began to take a more active role in the fighting. Helicopter gunships flown by American pilots ferried South Vietnamese troops into and out of battle zones. American aircraft dispensed herbicides and defoliants in Communist-controlled areas, poisoning food crops and destroying the jungle cover. At times advisers accompanied South Vietnamese troops on combat missions."[15]*

In May of 1964, I finished high school and left for the Navy three short days after high school graduation ceremonies. I met up with a high school buddy, Dan, who had enlisted at the same time. We departed Albuquerque by train, headed for Chicago and the Great Lakes Naval Training Facility, north of Chicago, Illinois.

I had never been on a train or airplane before. I slept the first night in the fold-out overhead Pullman bed and ate in the dining car. I was impressed with this mode of travel. After transferring trains in Chicago, we arrived at the induction center the next evening, long after the chow hall had closed. We had not eaten for several hours, so we requested some food. The two of us were promptly marched over to the darkened mess hall, where the cleaning crew managed to find a loaf of bread and a stick of bologna. I ate the bread.

The first few days were a whirlwind. Constant pressure, strip naked, put everything except your ID into a box to be shipped home. Initial issue of "skivvies" to hide your nakedness and then a week of the first phase of your life transformation. Your head was shaved, multiple medical vaccinations; didn't matter if you had been inoculated for smallpox, polio, and the like, you were getting it again. Initial clothing issue, stencil your name on your new clothes, wash your new clothes, by hand of course. Constant IQ, aptitude, and physiological testing to establish where the Navy thought you would best fit in, regardless of your own goals and aspirations.

---

14 *Vietnam: A History of the War.* Russell Freedman, Page 53, Holiday House, 1956
15 Ibid, page 55

Somewhere in the process I was joined up with 60 or so other recruits to form a "Company." This was the start of discipline indoctrination. I recall one poor soul who still thought he had a voice in matters and decided to resist. Within seconds, a senior first-class boatswains mate appeared out of nowhere, grabbed the kid, and dragged him off behind a nearby barracks. After several minutes they reappeared, the young recruit obviously the worst for wear. That night, laying in my top bunk, after lights out, I recall reflecting to myself, "What have I done?" I buried my head in my pillow and sobbed silently and uncontrollably for several minutes.

In those days, the Great Lakes Naval Training facility was divided into two distinct areas, separated by the main railroad running between Chicago, Illinois, and Milwaukee, Wisconsin. The east section included the base command and induction facilities; the west side was the training facility. After about five days we packed our sea bags with everything that the Navy had issued to us to begin our new identity and life. Sea bags over our shoulders, we marched through the railroad train underpass to confront what we all knew was going to be 12 weeks of hell. We also knew that not everyone would successfully complete the training.

After several weeks, which included constant marching, close-order drills, firefighting school, the tear gas house, more shots, more tests, hand-scrubbing your clothes, inspections, more inspections, the subject of my going to the Annapolis Naval Academy surfaced.

It was early evening and we were busy getting ready for the next day's personal and clothing inspections. I was at the wash table, scrub brush in hand, diligently scrubbing the brown stripes from my skivvies when that infamous first-class boatswains mate appeared asking for "Coen." Having observed him in action several weeks previously, I knew he was not a person to trifle with; I answered the call. As I stood at attention before him in my skivvies, he inquired, "I understand you are supposed to go to Annapolis." I replied, "Yes sir". He then instructed me to prepare a three-page paper explaining the reasons for desiring this assignment. The paper was to be submitted at the next morning's muster. Returning to the wash table to continue preparation for the next morning's inspection, I contemplated my plight. First, I didn't have three pieces of blank paper. Second, Annapolis had been my recruiter's idea, not mine. That was the last time the Navy and I discussed Annapolis.

A few weeks later, we finally got our first clue as to what our future in the Navy might look like. We each received a rate classification, which was a result of all the previous testing. I had requested as my first choice "engineman," the closest thing to a mechanic I thought the Navy might have. My high-test scores had followed me again. The Navy decided that I would be best as an aviation machinist mate. I was slated to attend the Navy's Jet engine mechanics school in Memphis, Tennessee, following completion of boot camp. With the future now defined, the anxiety level began to subside, and our thoughts turned to graduation and two weeks' home leave. Of course, the Navy had to give us one final parting shot: shaved head one week before going home!

On a rainy day in early August 1964, having successfully completed Navy Basic training, I boarded the train and headed back to Santa Fe for two weeks leave. It was good to be home, although all my high school classmates had scattered so there wasn't much to do except parade around in my Navy "dress blues," despite the boot camp haircut.

Figure 5: Home from Boot Camp

5

THE VIETNAM WAR

President Johnson's military advisers urged him to authorize air strikes against North Vietnam, and if necessary to send American combat troops. Other Johnson aides advised caution, warning that the growing U.S. involvement in Vietnam might bring Communist China into the conflict, triggering World War III.... Through long hours of discussions, Johnson listened to all points of view. He agonized over the decision he had to make. The war Johnson really wanted to fight was the war against poverty and inequality in the United States.... Johnson worried that the growing involvement in the war in Vietnam would drain America's resources and divert attention from his ambitious domestic program.... And yet the president felt that he could not abandon the American commitment to South Vietnam. He could not back down.... In Johnson's mind, nothing could be as terrible as the thought of being responsible for America's losing a war to the Communists. Nothing would be worse than that.[16]

Johnson was determined not to 'lose' South Vietnam to Communism. But he wanted 'to seek the fullest support of congress for any major action that [he] took.' So, while he resisted calls to unleash a bombing campaign, he increased the number of U.S. military advisers to 23,000. And he approved a secret plan for raids against the North Vietnamese coast by South Vietnamese naval commando units under U.S. control. As the attacks began, fast torpedo boats bombarded Communist radar sites and other coastal installations, while South Vietnamese commandos were landed by sea to blow up rail and highway bridges near the coast.

In August 1964, a strange incident off the northern coast led to a dramatic escalation of America's role in the Vietnam War. President Johnson received reports that two U.S. Navy destroyers had been attacked by North Vietnamese torpedo boats in the Gulf of Tonkin, apparently in retaliation for the sabotage campaign Johnson had approved earlier that

---

16 *Vietnam: A History of the War.* Russell Freedman. Pages 64-68, Holiday House 1956

year. And yet details about the reported attacks did not seem to add up. Neither U.S. vessel was damaged. No American was injured…. Despite the uncertainties, Johnson ordered the first U.S. air strikes against North Vietnam in retaliation for what he claimed was 'open aggression on the high seas.' And he asked Congress to give him the power to take additional military action as he saw fit.[17]

It is hard to say at what moment South Vietnam's struggle against Communist subversion and invasion became an American war, for we were drawn in gradually rather than at one dramatic stroke. But perhaps it became the Navy's war on a hot Sunday afternoon in August 1964, when North Vietnamese torpedo boats charged over the horizon at 50 knots and energetically tried to sink the destroyer Maddox 30 miles out to sea in the Gulf of Tonkin. Narrowly evading the torpedoes, the Maddox slammed a five-inch shell into one of the attackers before jets whistled up from the Ticonderoga, arrived to drive off the attackers with rockets and cannon fire. Two nights later the torpedo boats came again in rain and haze, with similar results. This time the Maddox, accompanied by the C. Tuner Joy, fought a running battle for several hours, dodging a swarm of torpedoes and sinking two torpedo boats.[18]

On August 7, Congress overwhelmingly passed the Tonkin Gulf Resolution, which authorized the president "to take all necessary measures to repel any armed attack against the forces of the United States and to prevent further aggression.[19]

I recall that on the evening of August 7, 1964, as recruits looking to graduate in three days, we listened to a smuggled transistor radio as Congress passed the Tonkin Gulf Resolution. We knew things had changed for all of us! Little did I know that within a few short weeks I would receive orders assigning me to Attack Squadron 56, which was currently aboard *Ticonderoga* in the Gulf of Tonkin. First, I would have to complete jet engine mechanics training in Memphis, Tennessee.

I had joined the Navy on May 21, 1964, oblivious to world events and optimistic that I would be cruising the Mediterranean in just a few short months. How quickly my fortunes had changed.

The Vietnam War becomes "Official"

On Sunday, August 2, 1964, aircraft from carriers *Ticonderoga* and *Constellation* were called to defend destroyers *Maddox* and *Turner Joy* who reported being under attack from North Vietnamese armed torpedo boats. The torpedo boat attack was neutralized, and all aircrews returned safely.

17 *Vietnam: A History of the War.* Russell Freedman, pages 68-69, Holiday House, 1956
18 *The Compact History of The United States Navy, new and revised edition.* Revised by Commander Hartley E. Howe, U.S.N.R., Hawthorn Books, Inc., September 1967
19 *Vietnam: A History of the War.* Russell Freedman, page 68-69

On the night of Tuesday, August 4, 1964, aircraft from the carrier *Ticonderoga* were launched to defend a supposed attack against the destroyers *Maddox* and *Turner Joy*. Aviators' immediate accounts of action are unable to confirm the existence of a credible attacking force. Defensive ordinance was discharged from ship and aircraft responding to "radar sightings." Unusual atmospheric conditions existed in the region that night and were later believed to have contributed to confusing shipboard battle control directions. No casualties or damage was reported.

On Wednesday, August 5, 1964, aircraft squadrons aboard carriers *Ticonderoga* and *Constellation* were notified to prepare for attacks against a PT-boat base and the oil storage facilities in the city of Vinh. The operation was considered as a reprisal for "the previous night's attack."

Vice Admiral James Stockdale, who survived 7 1/2 years as a POW in North Vietnam, remembers preparing for the missions of August 5, 1964, in his book *In Love and War*. As commander of Fighter Squadron 51 aboard *Ticonderoga*, he writes,

> *I felt like I was one of the few men in the world who really understood the enormity of what was going to happen. The bad portents of the moment were suffocating. We were about to launch a war under false pretenses, in the face of the on-scene military commander's advice to the contrary. This decision had to be driven from way up at the top. After all, I'd spent the summer reading messages setting up our Laos operations and I had grown familiar with linkages. It was all straight shot: Washington, Saigon, Ambassador Vientiane. On-scene naval officers couldn't turn that on or off any more than they could this thing now. There is no question of coming up with the truth from out here. The truth is out. Even a small potato like me is on the wire with a straight report of "no boats."*

> *The fact that a war was being conceived out here in the humid muck of the Tonkin Gulf didn't bother me so much; it seemed obvious that a tinderbox situation prevailed here and that there would be war in due course anyway. But for the long pull it seemed to me important that the grounds for entering war be legitimate. I felt it was a bad portent that we seemed to be under the control of a mindless Washington bureaucracy, vain enough to pick their legitimacies regardless of evidence.*

> *It was afternoon when we manned our planes. As we left the ready room, we were told that an hour before, the President had announced on national television that we would be striking North Vietnam targets. That struck fear in my heart because surprise was so important to the Spads' safety on this mission.*[20]

---

20 *In Love and War: The Story of a Family's Ordeal and Sacrifice during the Vietnam Years.* Jim and Sybil Stockdale, Harper & Row Publishers, 1984, pgs. 24-29

The Navy in Vietnam

As a naval action, Tonkin Gulf was insignificant; as the trigger for increased American involvement in Vietnam, it was history. Under direct orders from the President, American planes bombed out the North Vietnam torpedo-boat base, sinking 25 of the boats. Later that week Congress passed a resolution giving the President power to take all necessary measures to repel any armed attack against forces of the United States and to prevent further aggression. By November the Marines were going ashore in South Vietnam in response to a Communist attack on an American airbase, and from then on American intervention in the war mounted rapidly.

Like Korea, Vietnam was basically a land war in which American troops were able to fight far from home because American sea power controlled the seven thousand miles between San Francisco and Saigon. But even more than Korea, the Navy had plenty to do right on the spot. As the fighting ashore grew in intensity, so did the Navy's operation in air, along the coasts, and up the rivers.

In February 1965 the United States initiated continuing air strikes against Vietnam. By this time most of the Seventh Fleet was concentrated in the South China Sea, and carrier-borne aircraft flew thousands of sorties. Their targets were the suspected Vietcong concentrations in the south, and the roads, rail lines, and bridges in North Vietnam on which Communist men and supplies rolled south to support the Cong. The number of carriers in the Seventh Fleet increased steadily. In September 1965 planes from three Seventh Fleet carriers were flying joint missions.

In December 1965, nuclear ships went into combat for the first time when the *Enterprise* arrived off Vietnam, accompanied by the nuclear-powered guided-missile frigate *Bainbridge.* By the end of the year there were five carriers on the station. Navy aircraft were carrying out as many as 150 sorties every day, and the pressure was kept up. As the war dragged on, the list of North Vietnam targets grew to include heavily defended oil storage tanks, power stations, and railyards close to Hanoi, North Vietnam's capital, and Haiphong, its port city. Losses mounted too—primarily from ground-to-air missiles and anti-aircraft fire. The enemy's Russian-built MIG's generally steered clear of the attackers; when they came up against Navy fighters they were usually shot down.[21]

---

21 *The Compact History of The United States Navy, new and revised edition.* Revised by Commander Hartley E. Howe, U.S.N.R Hawthorn Books, Inc September 1967

My last Training Hurdle

Following my two-week Boot Camp Leave, I prepared for my next assignment, Jet Engine Mechanics School. At the appointed time, Mom and the kids drove me down to Lamy, where I caught the train for Memphis, Tennessee.

Aviation Machinist Mate "A" school was great. It was about 16 weeks long, and I had one basic responsibility: study and pass the coursework. It was a bit of an adjustment, transitioning from a seaman recruit to a real Navy man. Occasionally, we got to rub shoulders with some senior men returning from deployment. This was the first real confirmation we got that what was going on in Vietnam was real and that I would end up participating. I enjoyed Memphis and the surrounding area. I had about as much fun as an 18-year-old without a car can have.

Besides learning how to maintain jet engines, we got a lot of general aviation training including survival skills at sea. Part of that training included suiting up in a parachute harness and then jumping from the building roof into the swimming pool below. We had to be able to get out of the harness before we came to the surface or repeat the exercise. I made it first try. About midway through the training we began to receive orders for our next duty assignment. My orders were to report to an A-4 Skyhawk training squadron at Naval Air Station, Lemoore, California. I was to continue "on the job training" with Training Squadron 125 until my ultimate assigned squadron, Attack Squadron 56, returned from Western Pacific Deployment, (Navy speak for Vietnam).

Letters from home indicated that things were not going well. My father was not paying his child support, Mom was struggling to make ends meet with her job as a cosmetic salesperson at the local Payless drug store. At this point I was an E-2 and made about $86 a month. I started sending $50 a month home to try and help. It sounded like my brother Richard, age 13, and sister Bobbie, age 16, were contributing to the stress as Mom tried to deal with the two younger siblings, Patty, age 7 and Tom, age 4. In mid-December,1964, I completed my training, sewed on my Airman-ADJ Striker stripe, and headed home for Christmas leave in route to Lemoore, California. By now I had learned that Airline Military Standby was the way to travel, so I flew home, my first airplane experience.

I arrived home in Santa Fe the week before Christmas 1964, and was stunned. I suspected things might be a little dire, but nothing like what I encountered. The refrigerator was empty, except for a half carton of milk. Preparations for Christmas were not even being considered. I had drawn 30 days' advance pay for my leave and had a little money, so I set about trying to restore some semblance of a normal home. Grocery shopping was the first order followed by an excursion into the hills to chop a Christmas tree. I then began shopping, trying to ration my money as best I could and still make sure everyone had a Christmas along with a roasted turkey dinner.

While at home, I spent some time down at the local Shell service station where I had worked nights and weekends before graduation. Jack, the owner, kept me in beer (I was still underage). The government thought I was old enough to die for my country, but not old enough to drink alcohol?

My high school mentor and auto mechanics teacher, Polo Sena, was there. Mr. Sena was a Navy veteran himself, having served in Korea, so I enjoyed sitting with him and talking Navy.

Christmas leave came and went, and it was time to catch a plane for California and another great unknown. I left Mom and the kids with a great deal of apprehension. I wasn't sure how she was going to survive financially. She was still having to borrow from relatives, had sold some jewelry, including her old wedding ring, to a pawn shop. Things at home looked very desperate to me.

I finally caught up with Attack Squadron 56 at Lemoore Naval Air Station, California, in early 1965 when they returned to the States. By September 1965 I was headed to the Tonkin Gulf, where I spent most of the next two years working the flight decks of carriers *Ticonderoga* and *Enterprise* as part of Attack Squadron 56.

6

My War

I arrived at Lemoore Naval Air Station the first week of January 1965. NAS Lemoore is located about 45 miles southwest of Fresno, California. Commissioned in 1961. At that time, NAS Lemoore was the newest and largest Master Jet Base in the Navy and home to almost all of the Navy's attack aircraft squadrons assigned to the Pacific Fleet.

Unlike the Navy bases I had experienced up to this point, at NAS Lemoore everything was new. WWII wooden barracks buildings were replaced with 2-and-3-story concrete barracks buildings with elevators, modern restrooms, and laundry facilities. At the "dining hall," you ate off individual plates and bowls, not metal trays. I was impressed. The aircraft landing strips, hangars, and maintenance facilities were located about 20 miles from the housing, barracks, and base exchange facilities. This separated the almost constant airplane noise from living accommodations.

I reported for duty to the "officer of the deck" of Attack Squadron 125 (VA 125) and immediately began orientation as to my immediate and future responsibilities. Included was a security briefing on what was happening in Vietnam and what my potential future role would be. At that point all doubt was removed; I was in "it."

VA 125 was a training squadron, permanently assigned to NAS Lemoore for familiarization training and equipping pilots, maintenance, and ground crews on the A4C and A4E attack aircraft. This period lasted at least 60 days, and then you were expected to move on to your assigned squadron. In my case, I had been assigned to Attack Squadron 56, which was still deployed on "WestPac" (Western Pacific/Vietnam). They were not expected to return for another 90 days.

Although I had successfully completed Jet Engine Mechanics School in Memphis, I soon found out that working as a jet engine mechanic was a long way off. There were lots of hurdles to jump first. My first "on the job" training involved learning how to perform the duties of a plane captain. Initially, I did not consider this assignment to be much more than grunt work because, yes, it involved a lot of washing and scrubbing airplanes. Later I began to appreciate the real role, importance, and necessity of the "brown shirted" plane captain. Duties included preflight inspection of your assigned aircraft, presence in the cockpit anytime the aircraft was moved to "ride the brakes," assisting the pilot with final preflight inspection, strapping the pilot into the cockpit, arming the pilot's emergency egress systems and oxygen breathing system, assist with starting the engine, coordinating with the pilot to confirm the proper function of all flight control systems while under power, arming all landing gear systems, and turning the aircraft and pilot over to ground control personnel for takeoff coordination. These duties were taught for both ground and carrier shipboard operations. New maintenance personnel, regardless of specific training, usually spend at least 12–18 months working as a plane captain.

In early February 1965, VA-125 was notified that VA-56 was back in residence at Lemoore and that most of the squadrons members had returned from the customary 30-day leave period. I was then transferred to my permanent duty assignment.

When a squadron takes up operations aboard ship or ashore, several members of the squadron are temporarily assigned to the "ship's company" to work in the galley as mess cooks or the barracks/berthing space as compartment cleaners or, aboard ship, in the ship's laundry. As a "newbie," I was in line for one of the assignments, which usually lasted 4–6 months. I was being considered for mess cooking, which I was not happy about. Fortunately, at the last minute another newbie volunteered, and I was spared. I was assigned to the line division as a plane captain.

The squadron had just returned from WestPac aboard the *USS Ticonderoga*. They had participated in the Gulf of Tonkin incident along with other bombing operations that followed.

Men assigned to the line division were some of the younger men of the squadron and very impressionable. This was not lost on the older men of the division, who enjoyed ridiculing, tormenting, and terrorizing us new guys. The "perils of the flight deck" was a favorite topic of conversation. The "salts" loved to tell about exploits that were still fresh on their minds. Around-the-clock flight quarters during the Gulf of Tonkin incident. Taking "little white pills" to keep awake while at flight quarters. The sailor who was killed on the flight deck after walking into a propeller while at night flight quarters.

With the squadron now at full strength, both pilots and enlisted, training began in earnest. We were notified that we would be deploying sometime in August aboard the *Ticonderoga* again. My anxiety level was increasing, and I was beginning to become terrified of the carrier flight deck. All the while, I was concentrating on learning my duties as a plane captain.

The pilots flew a full schedule daily, dropping practice bombs at gunnery ranges near Fallon, Nevada, and 29 Palms, California. It was on one of these days that a previously launched sortie came back one plane and pilot short. We were told the executive officer, CDR Tigner, had made a run on a target and failed to pull out of the dive. He ejected at the last minute, but it was too late; he was too close to the ground. An accident investigation team was assembled, which included pilots and maintenance personnel, to visit the crash site.

The following Monday, after the team had returned, we came to work and entered the "line shack," as it was called. Sitting in the middle of the room was the wreckage of the ejection seat, the significance of which was not lost on me. A couple of the older, less tactful plane captains began bragging about what the burned ejection seat really meant and how death could be just around the corner for any one of us. Within a couple of days, a memorial service was held at the base chapel, attended by all hands as well as pilots and their wives. The whole experience shook me at my roots. I recall after leaving the chapel, taking a very long walk to regain my composure. I then knew, for certain, that "this was for real." A few days after the memorial service, we did our first TAD, temporary active duty, to Fallon, Nevada, for gunnery and bombing practice.

As a side note, our squadron's primary mission was nuclear weapons delivery. Technicians were never sure if the A-4 aircraft could escape the nuclear weapon blast following delivery. To counter this issue, they developed a procedure known as "lob bombing." The aircraft would run on the target, pull up and turn back inverted, releasing the bomb just as the plane turned vertical. By then retracing the course they hoped the plane and pilot could survive and clear the blast area. I got to visit the bomb range and tracking station as they were practicing this maneuver, and it was very interesting.

In the middle of this deployment, a detail was dispatched to Point Loma, California, the Rosecrans National Cemetery, to inter CDR Tigner. I volunteered for the assignment. We flew to San Diego, California and buried CDR Tigner with full Military Honors. The reality of my situation was beginning to soak in. My first real life experience with death and tragedy.

Within a few weeks, the squadron packed up for another TAD, two weeks of carrier qualifications aboard the *Ticonderoga* out of San Diego, California. The enlisted and maintenance personnel flew to North Island Naval Air Station. The pilots ferried the planes there also. During our brief stay at North Island Naval Air Station, I took the test for third class petty officer. Results would be published in a couple of months.

The planes were loaded aboard ship by crane, and out to sea we went. This was my first shipboard experience and first time working the flight deck. As a plane captain (brown shirt), I had an airplane assigned to me and it was my responsibility, unless it was flying. Plane captains spend 12–15 hours per day with their assigned aircraft. In addition to the constant inspections, "brown shirts" check fluid levels, prepare the cockpit for flight, and ensure there is no foreign object debris that could damage the "bird." Prior to handing the aircraft over to the pilot, the plane captain acts as the final set of eyes. Plane captains are usually the most junior personnel in the squadron. However, they are taught that they are responsible for the pilot's life and a multimillion-dollar aircraft. Combine that with the fact that the flight deck of an aircraft carrier is one of the most dangerous places on earth, I was terrified.

The two weeks passed quickly. The new pilots were practicing carrier launch and recovery, day and night, and as plane captains we were learning new skills as well. As I recall, this period was during the middle of summer and it was very hot. It was even hotter below decks in the berthing compartments. I took to sleeping curled up in the cockpit of my plane, after flight quarters had secured—not very conducive to restful sleep.

The *Ticonderoga* was an old Essex-class carrier. There was a bronze plaque in the island structure, commemorating the four Kamikaze attacks she suffered during WWII. Obviously, air conditioning for enlisted men's berthing areas was nonexistent.

We completed our second TAD assignment without incident and headed back to Lemoore. I was more convinced than ever that I wanted no part of the flight deck, so I started immediately to lobby for a position in the jet engine shop. I knew a vacancy was coming up, and I was the senior aviation machinist mate "striker" in the squadron.

Within a month, a TAD assignment became available at the Lemoore Quick Engine Exchange (QEC), facility. This was a facility run by the Naval Air Station, where new replacement jet engines are taken out of their steel pressurized container and all the operational components are added to the engine before a test run at the adjoining test cell. Once completed, the engine is ready for swapping whenever one of the various squadrons needed to replace a malfunctioning engine. This was a substantial opportunity for me, and it might keep me off the flight deck when we eventually deployed. I got along very well with the other mechanics, and they promised to put in a good word for me when it was time to go back to the squadron.

Finding and Questioning my Faith

Shortly after my arrival at Lemoore Naval Air Station and hooking up with Attack Squadron 56, I was approached by a man, Karl, from a neighboring squadron who inquired about my interest in Bible study. The only Bible I owned was a small New Testament that had been given out in boot camp. He offered to loan me a Bible if I would care to join him in study. Up until this time I had not been exposed to any meaningful religious experience. My father felt that as children we should be free to make our own choice. He was raised Catholic and later in life had chosen not to follow that path. Unfortunately, as kids, we were never exposed to any religious teaching from which to form an opinion.

I accepted Karl's invitation and for several months during the summer of 1965, I would meet with Karl at 6:00 a.m., two days a week, and sit inside his car outside the base barracks building for 30–45 minutes of spiritual fellowship. We would read the Bible, recite verses that we had memorized, and end with prayer. It wasn't very long before I accepted Christ as my Lord and Savior and I got serious about becoming a committed Christian.

Individual prayer was a new concept for me. Initially Karl suggested that I pray for what was on my mind. If I had a special need, to make God aware of that need. At that point in my life I had few needs, but lots of desires. Taking Karl's advice to heart, I started earnest prayer for fulfillment of desires—a temporary duty assignment to Albuquerque, New Mexico, assignment to the jet shop, etc.— all of which ended up being categorized as "unanswered prayers."

My association with Karl and our extracurricular spiritual commitments soon became known by a few within the squadron who then chose to make my activities a subject of ridicule and taunting. I learned to keep my religious faith to myself and thus became a "closet Christian." In the fall of 1965, my squadron was deployed, and I left my friend Karl behind in California. By this time, I had gotten serious about my faith, had bought my own Bible, and began to read religious-oriented material.

Prior to being deployed, I had visited my uncle David Potter in Santa Barbara, and he advised me that if I was planning to go to college after the Navy, I should start to prepare myself by reading, anything and everything. I then began to develop the habit of always carrying a pocket book with me and reading whenever I had the chance. One of the first books I read was *Dear and Glorious Physician* by Taylor Caldwell. I enjoyed this book very much and it wasn't until I was well into the book that I realized it was about Saint Luke. This was an eye opener for me, to learn that a novel could be fun to read and informative.

Around the first of August 1965, the squadron was getting ready for the upcoming deployment, and it was time for me to rejoin them. The big question was: Would I have to go back to the line division as a plane captain, or would they assign me to the jet shop? The head of the QEC shop went over to the squadron and spoke with PO1 Fuller, the head of the jet shop. He must have really talked me up as I was immediately welcomed back to the squadron as part of the jet shop. We once again prepared to embark aboard the *USS Ticonderoga*, home ported in North Island, San Diego. We spent about a week in San Diego getting settled in, bringing the planes aboard, etc.

Finally, September 28, 1965, that fateful day, arrived. As part of the "Man the Rail" detail, I stood, along with several hundred other sailors, in my dress whites as we prepared to cast off. Family members and civilians had been asked to disembark and were gathered below on the pier. Then the ship's chaplain asked for a moment of prayer. I will never forget those few moments, knowing that some of us would not be returning, and that we had enough nuclear weapons aboard to blow half the world away. The chaplain was asking for God's help in our "mission." The incongruity of asking for God's help with waging war was not lost on me. The first cracks in my newfound religious faith began to appear. Little did I know that I was on the verge of a "crisis of faith" that would last some 25 years.

My War Commences

We got underway. I was safely away from the flight deck, tucked into the mechanic's shop on the hangar deck just forward of the fantail. Our first stop would be Hawaii, where we would undergo five days of intense operational readiness inspection (ORI).

The crossing was uneventful. We noticed that as we got closer to Hawaii, the sea color turned from deep blue to an emerald green. The air temperature became more temperate. At last we spotted land and Captain Miller spoke over the 1-MC congratulating the ship's navigator for excellent course charting. We waited outside Pearl Harbor overnight before easing into the carrier pier alongside Ford Island on October 4, 1965. We tied up directly astern of the *USS Utah*, which remains on its side following the attack on Pearl Harbor in 1941.

Prior to arrival in Hawaii, we were all briefed on the HASP, Hawaiian Armed Services Police. This was a multiservice military police group, which did not tolerate misbehavior by servicemen on liberty. We were told that these men dealt with any infraction, especially underage drinking, swiftly and forcefully. Fresh from this briefing, liberty was arranged over the next three days so that all hands got a quick day's liberty in Honolulu.

We stayed alongside Ford Island for about four days before beginning our ORI. One afternoon, while alongside the Ford Island pier, I noticed quite a bit of activity down on the pier. On closer inspection, I observed a large nuclear weapons movement operation taking place. Weapons were being offloaded from the ship by crane and other weapons were being brought aboard. I hypothesized that the ship's armory was being updated with the latest version. Everything was being done with tight security under cover of tarps to shield the activity from any passing overhead satellites.

ORI began with the boarding of the inspection team, which consisted of several dozen individuals, most with no recognizable identification. The purpose of the ORI was to test the ship's and crew's readiness for combat or any of type emergency. The inspection team would set up a surprise scenario and then observe how the crew responded. We were graded, and theoretically a failing grade would prevent the ship and crew from proceeding on to our deployment objective.

We cast off from Ford Island and with the assistance of harbor tugs made the 180-degree turn and headed out to sea. As advertised, general quarters was sounded immediately and we began to respond to whatever situation the inspection team had invented. The drills were constant, anytime day and night. Man overboard, fire below decks, flight deck crash, air defense from attacking hostile aircraft, damage control to prevent flooding, and then of course, flight deck operations day or night where pilots had to respond to various midair and ground threats.

With the Operational Readiness Inspection satisfactorily completed and a few days of well-deserved liberty in Honolulu, on October 17, 1965, we set sail for the Philippines. We arrived in Subic Bay on the first of November 1965, for four days. The base had some very nice swimming and snorkeling areas, and of course every sailor had to experience the infamous town of Olongapo, just outside the gate. The good news was, there was no drinking age, so all could partake.

We then departed Subic Bay to begin the job we had come to do. Arriving off the coast of South Vietnam, we took up our assignment on Dixie Station and began combat operations in support of U.S. ground forces in the South. Shortly after we first arrived on our first Dixie Station assignment, we learned that all hands would be receiving combat pay for our time served in the war zone theater. This amounted to about $100 a month, so it was significant. About this time, I received notice that I was to be promoted to 3rd class Petty Officer, NCO status; this also resulted in a significant pay raise. In addition, the Navy instituted "hazardous duty pay" for persons working on the flight deck. This also was about $100 a month. I was beginning to rethink my aversion to working on the flight deck.

After about two weeks we rotated northward to Yankee Station and began missions against targets in the North. Tensions where high as we began handling live bombs and ammunition, flying shifts of 12–13 hours both night and day as required. Russian MiG's were operating over the North at that time and encounters were occasional, but we prevailed. Around the third of December we were relieved of combat duty and ordered to sail to Yokosuka, Japan, for a pre-Christmas liberty period of about a week, just long enough to get our Christmas shopping done.

As we steamed north toward Yokosuka, on December 5, 1965, the powers that be decided that a nuclear weapon loading exercise would be in order. These exercises were conducted very precisely and scripted methodically, and the weapon had a very deliberate chain of custody which must be followed. There were 6–8 loading teams with as many as 10 participants on each team, including an armed marine guard. Specific aircraft were designated for loading and were relocated to the hangar deck. The individual weapons were brought up by elevator from the magazine to the hangar deck and custody was turned over to the loading team. Following a very detailed and precise procedure, the weapon was loaded onto the aircraft and secured. Actual arming was simulated. A designated pilot was then summoned from the ready room to take control of the weapon and aircraft. With the assistance of the plane captain, the pilot was strapped into the cockpit and assumed a "ready for launch" demeanor. The aircraft, weapon, and pilot were then moved to the hangar deck elevator and raised to the flight deck. The loaded aircraft was then moved to one of the catapults and a launch sequence simulated. At this point the drill would end for that particular weapon, aircraft, and pilot. The weapon was offloaded and returned to the magazine.

The Disaster that "Never Happened"

December 5, 1965, was a day I will never forget. LTJG Douglas Webster had taken custody of his aircraft loaded with a B43 nuclear bomb. The aircraft handlers, moving the plane by hand, located the aircraft in front of the number 2 elevator and proceeded to push it out onto the elevator. The senior handler, Yellow Shirt, blew his whistle signaling the pilot to apply brakes so they could chain-tiedown the aircraft prior to raising it to the flight deck. The pilot did not respond. Frantic whistle blowing and screaming erupted to no avail. At the last moment, the pilot seemed to respond, was seen trying to raise himself out of the cockpit, but it was futile; he was strapped in. The plane continued to roll backwards, struck a short metal curb at the edge of the elevator, flipped backwards, belly up, and sank into the ocean.

I was on the hangar deck at the time, heard the commotion, and ran forward to the elevator just as the plane flipped over. Everyone around started throwing anything that would float overboard to mark the spot. "Man overboard" was called as we stood on the side and watched the bubbles rising, hoping against hope to see a head bob up, but there was nothing. Some of us just looked at each other wondering, "What the hell just happened?" Within a couple of minutes, the two empty exterior fuel tanks separated from the plane and bobbed to the surface. A motorized dingy with an EOD specialist was lowered over the side to search for wreckage, but all he could do was shoot holes in the drop tanks, so they would sink.

The International Code for a nuclear weapons accident is "Broken Arrow," and it must be communicated, in this case, to the Chief of Naval Operations within a very short prescribed time period. At some point that requirement was met by Captain Miller. LTJG Webster, the plane, and bomb were never recovered. Shortly thereafter the wreckage was located at a depth of 16,300 ft. about 80 miles from a remote Japanese Island.

Besides the obvious, this incident caused several very serious problems for the Navy. By treaty, U.S. nuclear armed or fueled ships were not allowed to enter Japanese waters. We were in violation of that provision. We were immediately advised by Captain Miller that we were not to discuss this incident with each other or anyone else. The incident "never happened"!

We arrived in Yokosuka the next day. At the pier, we were greeted by one of the largest contingents of black cars and high-ranking navy brass I think I have ever seen in one place.

As the story began to unfold further, we learned that the Navy had been unsuccessful in locating LTJG Webster's wife. As the Navy brass began to converge on the ship to convene an accident investigation process, somewhere in the crowd walking up the ship's gangway was Mrs. Douglas Webster, looking to surprise her husband and to share in his "Christmas leave" in Japan.

Besides the tragic loss of life, this event is characterized by many years of denial and deception on the part of the U.S. government. After 25 years, Greenpeace first publicly disclosed the events that only a few of us had known. It also came to light that after 18 years the U.S. State Department finally divulged the actual location of the incident, which had previously been misrepresented to the Japanese government.

Despite the shadow of that tragic event, most of us were able to enjoy Yokosuka. Christmas shopping including the requisite set of china to be sent home. Seiko watches were the order of the day, along with 35mm SLR cameras. Along with several of my shipmates, we boarded the trains to explore various places like Tokyo, Kamakura, the Giant Buddha, and Yokohama. It was a new world for many of us. This was the Navy I had envisioned. Like all good things, this too came to an end. On the 16th of December, we headed back to the line for another combat period.

Figure 6: The Giant Buddha at Kamakura

On the 22nd of December, we were honored by the presence of Martha Raye and her 65/66 Vietnam tour. What a show and what a lady! At the end of the show in the dark of night gathered on the flight deck, she asked us to join her in singing "Silent Night." There wasn't a dry eye in the house; I've never been able to sing that song since.

About a week later we were assigned "to close" Cam Ranh Bay from any outside insurgence attempt. The Bob Hope Christmas show was in-country, and their protection was a priority. Of course, the big payoff was that they would be coming aboard for a couple of days and would do a show on the flight deck.

December 29, 1965, Bob Hope and his Christmas tour entourage arrived, including Kaye Stevens, Anita Bryant, Linda Battsa (Miss USA World), Joey Heatherton, Carol Baker, Jack Jones, Nicholas Brothers, Jerry Colonna, and Peter Leeds. Their show was incredible and a huge boost to all in attendance. They spent a couple of days on board, touring the ship and visiting with crew members. Carol Baker even gave a couple autographs of her previously released *Playboy* spread.

Figure 7: Bob Hope and Carol Baker 1966

The last night they were aboard, they were having dinner in the wardroom. As the story was told to me, one of the ladies commented that she would like to see night flight carrier operations. The captain broke out a couple of fighter pilots, and flight quarters was sounded. The troupe assembled on the bridge and the show began. We launched a couple of F-8 fighters to circle the ship for a brief time. Of course, we also had to launch the rescue helicopter to stand by. The landing signal officers assembled back at the LSO platform to direct landing/recovery operations. While attempting to recover one of the F-8s, the pilot was too low and slammed into the "round down" at the stern of the flight deck. The plane exploded, the pilot ejected, and wreckage scattered across the flight deck and into the sea. The helicopter was able to rescue the F-8 pilot from the dark ocean, and he was brought aboard. All the while the bridge was screaming over the 1-MC, "Doctor to the flight deck! Doctor to the flight deck!" One of the landing gear struts that came off the exploding airplane had hit the LSO standing back on the platform. I was later told that it had split his head open.

Very soon afterwards you could feel the ship go to full power. I went up topside to poke around and assess the damage to several of the airplanes that had been parked alongside the recovery area. It soon became common knowledge that we were steaming at full speed to rendezvous with the hospital ship *Repose*. I stayed up on the flight deck until about 0300, when a helicopter was lowered to the hangar deck and the critically wounded LSO loaded aboard. The helicopter quickly took off into the night. Much later I learned that the LSO never regained consciousness and died about 30 days later. The military newspaper *Stars and Stripes* made a big deal about how the F-8 pilot had been rescued and survived. No mention was ever made of the death of the LSO. In Bob Hope's later book, *Five Women I Love*, he tells this story without mention of the death of the LSO. I have since identified him as Lt. Richard W Hastings. And so, the war went on.

We ended our rotation from Yankee Station with a week of liberty in Subic Bay, Philippines. We returned to Dixie Station in late January 1966, and after a couple of weeks rotated "up north" to Yankee Station.

Sailors are naturally superstitious, and aboard the Ticonderoga we believed tragedy came in threes. I don't recall the event that touched this sequence off, but I vividly remember the last two in the sequence. February 1, 1966, was a routine day of Operation Rolling Thunder strikes. As the returning flight of A-4's from VA-56 began to prepare for landing, flight leader LCDR Render Crayton requested a flyover to check if both main landing gear were down. The flight deck reported "negative"; one main gear was still retracted. It was decided that LCDR Crayton should try a "bump and run" across the flight deck to see if the gear could be jarred loose. This maneuver was unsuccessful. After much discussion and a "beach bingo" was ruled out, it was decided that a "wheels up barricade catch" was the only viable option. "Rig the barricade" was called on the flight deck, and crash crews sprang into action. Meantime the pilot began reducing the fuel load as much as possible to minimize fire danger on landing. The catch was letter perfect, a small amount of flame from the intake upon arrest, but LCDR Crayton had landed safely. The airplane was not in as good of shape. Event number 2!

Figure 8: Crayton takes the Barricade

One week later, on February 7, 1966, came event number 3. LCDR Crayton was not as lucky this time. The story is best told by LCDR Crayton's Wingman, Lt Ed Pfeiffer, as follows:

On February 6th, 1966, an American pilot returning from a bombing mission over North Vietnam was forced to bail out of his flak-damaged aircraft. He ejected from his crippled jet off Cape Falise, North Vietnam, landing in the Gulf of Tonkin within three miles of the enemy shoreline. The U.S. Rescue and Recovery forces dispatched a destroyer to pick him up. As the destroyer neared the downed airman, it came under fire from North Vietnamese shore batteries and torpedo boats, which were racing to beat the destroyer to the pilot. The destroyer fired back, driving off the torpedo boats, and momentarily silencing the shore batteries. The rescue effort was successful, but the shore batteries were well entrenched and would require more stringent measures to silence them permanently. An air strike was planned for the following day.

February 7 was a grey, gloomy day in the Gulf of Tonkin. Low dirty clouds filled the sky and visibility was extremely poor. On board the carrier Ticonderoga, five A-4E Skyhawks of VA-56 loaded with 500 lb. bombs, 2.75 rockets, and 20mm HEI for their twin cannon, were guided to the catapults. The flight leader was LCDR Render Crayton. His section leader was Lt. Ed Pfeiffer. One by one the Skyhawks were tensioned to the steam catapults, then slung off the bow of the carrier into the murky skies. Joining in loose combat formation, the flight leader headed west at 500 feet above the choppy waters of the South China Sea. The pilots strained for the first faint outlines of the enemy coast, five sets of eyes willing it to appear. They were within two miles of the shoreline before the keenest of those eyes spotted it. They spread the formation further, and banking right, began their search for the shore batteries. Crayton's navigation had been good, and within minutes the shore batteries slid out of the murk, passing in review off their left wings. Attack orders crackled in five seats of soft rubber earphones as Crayton set his A-4's up for the attack. Fingers danced over armament control panels, selecting ordnance to be dropped, charging guns, getting ready. The buttons and trigger on the control column were alive now, and five right hands adjusted their grips on the sticks. The clouds were scattered to broken and reached to within 1,000 feet of the ground. The Skyhawks would have to "pop up" into the crud, roll in, and pick up their targets as they dove out of the overcast. Not many jets would be agile enough to press an attack under these conditions, but Crayton was confident that their Skyhawks were, and could.

As Crayton screamed out of the clouds on his first pass, the enemy gun crews opened up with small arms fire. Each of the Skyhawks made a pass at the batteries, pressing to within 500 feet of the ground before dropping their bombs. The North Vietnamese ground fire built to a fever pitch, as the enemy gun crews fought to stave off the attackers. The bombers managed to destroy one gun and damage another in the first pass, but with the weather bad and worsening, Crayton decided to abandon their briefed target, in favor of targets in other clearer areas. Accordingly, he instructed Pfeiffer to take two of the A-4's and head north, while he and his wingman turned south in search of "targets of opportunity."

Pfeiffer and his two wingmen climbed to 3,000 feet and, jinking (flight maneuver) as they went, headed north. The minutes dragged by as they slid in and out of clouds, searching for enemy activity. One of the wingmen spotting a briefed landmark, called out a warning: "Watch out for this area, it's heavily defended!" Just then, Pfeiffer emerged from a cloud to be met by a murderous storm of AAA (flak). Shrapnel rattled off his fuselage as he broke hard right, heading for the Gulf of Tonkin, convinced that he had taken hits in the A-4's vitals. His two wingmen, having taken their own evasive action, lost him in the scramble to get out of the hot area. Miraculously, he was joined by Crayton, who had heard the radio calls, and turned seaward to help. The battery of warning lights on Pfeiffer's panel remained mute, as Crayton slid from one side of his mate's Skyhawk to the other, searching for evidence of flak damage. There was no apparent damage, so they decided to continue their search for NVA targets.

Upon reaching the coast, they turned south along the main north-south artery, Route 1. Immediately they spotted worthy targets. Crayton had some railroad rolling stock on a siding, and Pfeiffer an intact railroad bridge. They set up in a left-hand pattern around their targets, with Crayton leading. The weather, though far from ideal, was much better in this area, as they were intent on doing a thorough job on the targets. None of them spotted the well camouflaged AAA emplacements.

As Crayton rolled over and started down the steep incline of his bomb run, the enemy opened up with everything he had. The little Skyhawk was bracketed by angry gray and black smudges immediately, taking fatal hits in the engine. Crayton jettisoned his ordnance short of the target and broke for the coast, hoping that his A-4 would last until he could get "feet wet" over the Gulf of Tonkin.

Pfeiffer and the wingman, also under fire, climbed into the overcast and turned to join their stricken leader. Crayton's valiant Skyhawk rapidly lost its battle with time and distance, and Pfeiffer, still in the clouds heard him call, "My controls are frozen! I'm rolling inverted! I'm ejecting!" Within seconds Pfeiffer emerged from a cloud, just in time to see the A-4 crash with a brilliant flash of orange in a flooded paddy. He spotted Crayton, with a good chute, floating earthward. Cranking his A-4 into a tight orbit around Crayton, Pfeiffer switched his radio to the survival radio frequency, as Crayton landed on a riverbank. Almost immediately Crayton came up on the survival radio, with; I'm OK, Ed, but I think my arm is broken." Pfeiffer acknowledged, promising to remain in the area to oversee the rescue operation. Then he switched frequencies again, calling the air-sea rescue people to report the situation and request a helo. They responded by scrambling a helo from a destroyer and diverting an HU-16 and two A-1's that had been on call for just such an emergency. Just then the errant wingman rejoined them. Pfeiffer instructed him to monitor the air-sea rescue frequency, keeping track of the rescue force's progress toward their area, while he went back to the survival radio frequency. Crayton came on the air with; "Ed, there's three guys on a dike across the river shooting at me!" Pfeiffer, unable to spot the enemy, asked for instructions. Crayton, acting as FAC, called: "OK, Ed, come in on a heading of one nine zero degrees, two thousand feet, three hundred forty knots, and I'll direct." Pfeiffer set his A-4 up for the strafing run and started in. More instructions: "Roll in on a thirty-degree and charge your guns. OK, hold … hold … FIRE NOW!" The twin 20 mm cannon popped, and a stream of shells pouted toward the dike. Pfeiffer followed the tell-tale tracers as they arched earthward. Then he spotted the trio of enemy soldiers. His first bursts were high, and the NVA hardly paused in their efforts to pick off Crayton. On his next pass,

Pfeiffer's shells exploded all around the enemy, silencing them. The communists, well aware of the prize at stake, marshaled more forces and shortly Crayton was on the radio with, "Ed, there's some guys coming across the river in a boat to get me!" Pfeiffer spotted them immediately and roared in to the attack. This time he pickled a 500-pound bomb, which exploded close by the boat, sending up a huge geyser of dirty brown water, swamping the boat and sending the survivors floundering for cover on the opposite riverbank.

Just as Pfeiffer was beginning to become concerned about his dwindling ammunition, the two A-1 Skyraiders showed up. The sight of the lumbering bomb-laden Spads reassured everyone on the scene. They felt they could now cope with whatever the enemy threw at them in the short time until the helo arrived for the pick-up. The NVA, realizing that someone would be coming for Crayton shortly, decided on an all-out attempt to capture him before the Americans could rescue him. Small communist patrols began to close on Crayton from all sides. The airwaves crackled as the American pilots exchanged instructions and comments on their repeated attacks at these thrusts. Their number one cheerleader, Crayton, urged them on, directing them from his increasingly untenable position.

By now the helo was long overdue. Pfeiffer, climbing to altitude between attacks, called him on the radio and was appalled to learn that the helo was apparently lost! The helo crew, monitoring the radio, had heard Pfeiffer's conversation with Crayton regarding the abortive communist attempt to cross the river in a boat. They had assumed that the downed pilot was floating in the Gulf of Tonkin, and were orbiting on the correct azimuth, but short of the coastline. Pfeiffer, choking back his anger, reaffirmed their position and urged the helo to get to them posthaste. Though out of ammunition, he dove back into the attack pattern. Pressing in dangerously close to the ground, he roared low over an enemy patrol, jettisoning his empty wing tanks, hoping to take some of them out as the tanks smashed into the ground. The enemy, perhaps sensing his frustration, continued to close on Crayton. On his next pass, Pfeiffer dropped his bomb racks. Still the communists pressed in toward Crayton. Pfeiffer had one all-consuming thought: he must protect his squadron leader until the helo arrived. He had only one weapon left, his airplane. He pushed the throttle to full military power and dove for the ground. Leveling off a few feet above the placid paddies, he charged at the communists at over 500 miles per hour. They saw him coming and flattened themselves, too surprised to fire at him. He flashed past, scant inches from them. They were stunned, but only momentarily, as they jumped to their feet and sprinted toward Crayton. He hauled on the stick, bending the nimble A-4 into a 6G turn, frantic to get back at the enemy before they could get to Crayton. As he commenced his second attack, the helo arrived on the scene. With rotor blades thrashing the humid air, it made straight for Crayton. The communists, ignoring Pfeiffer, directed the full force of their fire at the advancing helo. It was hit immediately, and often. The enemy was now within a few yards of Crayton and he realized the hopelessness of the situation. He knew that Pfeiffer and his wingman were dangerously low on fuel and made a final transmission; "Well, Ed, I can see them now ... they're almost on top of me ... they all have guns ... thanks for a good try ... you guys better go home." Pfeiffer made a last low pass, then, with communist small arms fire chasing him, climbed toward the coast. He didn't know if he had been hit or not. He was well below "bingo fuel." And if he didn't find an A-3 tanker, he would be swimming in the South China Sea before too long. But all of these things seemed insignificant next to the realization that NVA had captured his friend and squadron leader. Pfeiffer and his wingman plugged into an A-3 at 20,000 feet and after filling up with JP, headed for Danang. The landing at Danang was uneventful. Careful inspection of his A-4 revealed no major damage, and he returned to the Ticonderoga.[22]

Back on board the *Ticonderoga* we recovered the remnants of Crayton's flight group as well as the two Skyraiders from VA-52. Although not mentioned by LT Pfeiffer, who obviously had his hands full, the Skyraiders had done everything they possibly could to save Crayton. This was evident in the battle damage that each aircraft suffered. The small arms bullet holes in the propellers along with numerous bullet holes throughout the airplane fuselages spoke to the bravery and effort of everyone involved to affect a different outcome!

That day was a turning point for me in several ways. At lights out that night the ship's chaplain came on the 1MC with his usual evening prayer. That night, as the chaplain offered a prayer for Cmdr. Crayton in his "hour of need," we could only imagine the pain and horror that he must be experiencing, let alone what the next years would be like for him. At the close of the prayer, lying in my bunk, I silently sobbed, where was God and how could he really be involved in this mess? As the chaplain prayed, I began to think harder about the hypocrisy of it all. How did it make sense to ask God to "choose a side" in this conflict? I was unable to answer that question then, and to this day have been unable to do so.

Figure 9a: George M. Cohen–White Shirt Crew

By now I had been working on the flight deck during flight operations as a "green shirt" mechanic and "white shirt" troubleshooter. As a "white shirt" safety troubleshooter, one of my responsibilities during an aircraft launch was to meet the plane as it taxied up to the catapult. My job was to do a final check under the aircraft looking for any leaks or other

---

22 A-4 Skyhawk in Action, Lou Drendel, Squadron/Signal Publications, 1973

abnormalities. If everything was in order, I would scramble out from under the plane and give the catapult officer a "thumbs up," meaning the plane was ready to go. On one particular day, just as I was scrambling out from underneath, I happened to notice something awry with the starboard side 20mm cannon. A quick check verified that during taxi to the catapult, the gun had come loose from its mount. I signaled "thumbs down" to the cat officer, which was not something he wanted to see. The launch sequence was interrupted as the plane was disconnected from the catapult and taxied back to an elevator and moved to the hangar deck below for repair. In the meantime, the standby plane and pilot were moved into position for launch to replace the downed aircraft. Just another day on the flight deck!

I had managed to milk the safety troubleshooter gig for about two months to get the flight deck pay, but it looked like that was coming to an end as the shop chief tried to spread the opportunity around.

I was bored in the "jet shop" and enjoying the "action" on the flight deck, having worked through my previous fear. I then began to think about the money and what I might want to do in another 18 months when I would be discharged. I decided that I needed to start putting some money away in the event I chose to go to college after the Navy.

Around the second week of February, we headed to Subic Bay, Philippines, for well-deserved liberty following a rough line period on Yankee Station. The squadron maintained a "Beach Detachment" of about ten enlisted and one officer at Cubi Point Naval Air Station, Subic Bay. In the event of an incident while "on station," that would prohibit a damaged aircraft from landing safely back aboard the carrier, one of the "Bingo" destinations was Cubi Point. This was especially desirable if the airplane had suffered damage that could be repaired and Cubi was in range of the aircraft. The beach detachment could receive the aircraft and make the required repairs and the plane would return to the ship. One of the designated members of the detachment was always an engine mechanic. Prior to arriving at Subic Bay, the maintenance chief approached me and asked if I would like to stay behind with the detachment during the next line period. With much trepidation, I agreed.

Upon arrival in Subic, I packed up my necessary belongings and moved into a barracks building at the naval station. Nice two-bunk private room, dining hall, and liberty in Olongapo every night—what could be better? I immediately began to have second thoughts. Still being a naïve 19-year-old, I was live bait for some of my more senior "shipmates." It had become widely known that I was inexperienced in the "ways of the world." My "friends" were eager to correct that situation and Olongapo was just the place.

After about two days, while the carrier was still in port, I began to seriously consider my situation. First, I would be giving up "combat pay" because I would not be in the conflict zone. Second, what were my real moral values, and could I maintain them with the intense pressure to be "part of the gang"? After some very intense soul searching, I went to the maintenance chief and asked to be replaced and to go back aboard the ship. He of course had no trouble finding another volunteer.

Back in Action

Back aboard and headed back to the line, I began to further contemplate my situation. I was aware that there was a possible opening back in the line division as a plane captain. I raised my hand and even though I was now an NCO, the chief agreed to let me go back "on the roof." This allowed me to address my money woes because I would be drawing combat pay and hazardous duty pay together. This was an additional $200 a month; ironically, the same rate the front-line marines and grunts were getting in-country.

Aboard a deployed aircraft carrier, the flight deck serves as the workplace for hundreds of sailors. It has been characterized as the most dangerous 4½ acres on earth. Although fraught with danger, it is a place of beauty, skill, and timing. Many writers have called the activity that takes place on the flight deck a "ballet." When it comes to timing and interaction the comparison is apt, but keep in mind that some of the other "dancers" are lethal multi-ton aircraft that, at times, travel hundreds of miles per hour. The dance floor is a hot, stench-filled, steel deck that can be measured in acres and contains hundreds of hazards.

Figure 9b: Landing operations

The flight deck is filled with activity: aircraft taxiing, engines starting, people running, whistles blowing, and sirens wailing. It is so busy that everyone must maintain situational awareness at all times. Aircraft are launching and recovering, catapults are shooting no loads, mechanics are doing engine maintenance turns, people are respotting and parking aircraft, airplanes and helos are being fueled, and ordnance crews are handling ordnance. Each flight deck task has the potential to end in a mishap. Knowing flight deck rules, learning how to maneuver about the deck, and recognizing hand signals is critical.[23]

Being a plane captain on the *Ticonderoga* was no easy job. Besides navigating all the flight deck hazards, keeping the aircraft clean was a necessary and constant job all in itself. The *Ticonderoga's* boilers where fired by fuel oil, and each night the flues were "rapped" to clear the soot. This black ash would exhaust through the stack and cover the airplanes that were parked behind the island structure. If your plane was one of the lucky ones and there had been a dew drop, your plane would be covered with a slick black coating. The only remedy was a can of "waterless cleaner," half a bale of rags, and lots of elbow grease. However, I was determined. As the only NCO plane captain in the squadron, I would set the standard, and I did. My aircraft was always spotless, and mechanically fit. I was well known for being capable of conducting one of the best preflights that could be had.

After about 30 days and much grumbling from my fellow plane captains, the chief came to me one day and said that it really didn't look good having an NCO as a plane captain. Would I consider giving up my plane and taking a new job as crew leader, responsible for seven planes and their plane captains? I proudly agreed.

Heading Home for a Rest

Letters from home, mostly from my mother, kept me apprised of the home situation. Mother had sold her house in Santa Fe and moved to Albuquerque. She had gotten a much better job, and my dad was beginning to slowly repay the child support arrearages. Mom mentioned that, through a friend, she had met a man, Ed Woods, that she was dating. It sounded like things were beginning to stabilize on the home front, which was a tremendous relief for me.

Shortly thereafter we set sail for Sasebo, and our second visit to Japan. Prior to arriving in Sasebo, I was advised that my grandfather, George E. Coen, had passed away. There wasn't going to be a memorial service, so I didn't see any need to go home. Dad had him cremated and had a pilot fly over the Sangre de Christo Mountains north of Santa Fe and spread his ashes. The death of a

---

23 Flight Deck Awareness 5th Edition 2008

nearby relative meant I was not allowed on liberty alone, but that was seldom a consideration anyway.

My mother wrote that she and Ed Woods were considering marriage, which was a tremendous load off my back. She finally would have someone else to look after her. I took the occasion in Sasebo to call home and introduce myself to Ed. Ed was a former Marine with the Second Division. He had seen action on Saipan and had been part of MacArthur's Japanese occupation forces, stationed in Tokyo. He told me about being in Nagasaki when the ground was still hot from the bomb.

Liberty in Sasebo meant more shopping, and trips to ground zero in Nagasaki. Lots of pictures and touring all the historic sights. I really enjoyed Sasebo, it was one of my favorite foreign port calls.

Figure 10:
Nagasaki–Ground Zero

We left Sasebo and returned to the line via a short stay in Subic Bay. At this point, the days all seemed to run together. "Flight quarters" required plane captains to be up preflighting their aircraft an hour before the call. Flight quarters secured 12 hours later followed by a deck respot to get planes requiring maintenance down to the hangar deck and flight-ready planes to the flight deck for the next day's launch. If you were lucky, you would get six hours of sleep in a hot, stinky berthing compartment before it all began again. By now we plane captains had fully earned the respect to be called a "roof rat," someone who survives on caffeine, nicotine, and adrenaline.

By now, we were also beginning to anticipate the end of the cruise sometime in May. We had been advised that upon returning to Lemoore NAS we would transfer out of Carrier Air Group 5 to Carrier Air Group 9 and make our next deployment aboard the carrier *Enterprise*. Included in this change was the changeout of all our aircraft from A4-Es to A4-Cs. This change required substantial retraining, both for pilots and crew. The most significant part of this change was a change in aircraft engines from J52s to J65s. The reason for the change was explained: aboard *Enterprise*, fighter support would now be provided by F-4 Phantoms rather than F-8 Crusaders, and our A4Es would be better served aboard the smaller carriers.

We were also anticipating one more major port of call, Hong Kong. On April 4, 1966, via another short stay in Subic Bay, we anchored out in the harbor of Hong Kong for a five-day liberty call. Hong Kong is an amateur photographer's dream for its contrasts and brilliant colors, especially at night. Since many of us had recently acquired Japanese cameras, we were ready to put our skills to the test. Tailored suits were also the order of the day. I brought home two.

Figure 11: Hong Kong–Begging for coins alongside the ship

We returned to Yankee Station from Hong Kong for what was supposed to be a quick and easy 12-day tour before beginning our journey home via Yokosuka, Japan. As it turned out, it was anything but quick and easy. Our mission assignments were well up north, and our pilots had their hands full. As I recall, on the last six days the air group lost one plane each day. Every pilot was rescued. We were going home, all of us!

We began preparations for our journey home from Yokosuka by first loading aboard many severely damaged aircraft of every sort that were destined for repair facilities back in the states. It is timely to note that an aircraft carrier's main defense capabilities rest with its aircraft. The significance of this is that the damaged aircraft consumed a very large portion of the flight deck. We could still launch aircraft, but to recover these aircraft we would have to dispose of the damaged aircraft over the side. This became problematic after we left Yokosuka and headed for San Diego via the Great Circle Route. About two days out of Yokosuka in a dense fog, Air Defense identified a group of Russian Brown Bear Bombers on radar trying to locate us. At that time, it was the policy of the U.S. Navy not to permit a flyover of a carrier by a foreign nation. If the Brown Bears could locate us and attempt to fly over, we would be required to launch the two F-8 fighters that were sitting ready for launch on the catapults. They would then intercept the Russians and escort them from the area. Their eventual recovery back aboard ship would be a problem if the launch of an "Air Defense" mission was required. The ship and our destroyer escorts began a zig-zag evasion course that lasted several hours. Fortunately, the Russians finally gave up and went on their way.

The crossing took about seven days, during which time we were all busy packing up the squadron's tools and equipment as well as our own personal belongings in preparation to disembark the ship in San Diego.

May 13, 1966, we finally tied up at Ford Island, San Diego, California. I along with about 90 percent of the squadron and ship's company went ashore and dispersed for a long, well-deserved, 30 days leave. I spent my thirty days leave period at home in Albuquerque. I met my recently acquired stepfather, Edward Woods. What a wonderful experience! I now knew that family at home was in good hands and I could get on with my life.

My father was working at Los Alamos, New Mexico, as the county engineer. I took a couple of days to go visit him. I neglected to tell him I was coming, choosing to walk into his office unannounced in full dress white uniform, campaign ribbons and all. I was surprised at his reaction. Following a brief hug, he immediately left the room, face buried in his hands. He did not return for several minutes. I have reflected that this was one of the first times that my father showed that he was really proud of me.

I returned to Lemoore, and immediately began training on the J65 jet engine. After all, my primary rating was a jet engine mechanic even though I held on to my coveted position as a line division crew leader. I also took advantage of a previous offer from my uncle and aunt, Bo and Velma Potter. When I first got to Lemoore, nine months earlier, they had offered to give me a 1957 Ford "business coupe," which they no longer had use for. I had declined their offer, fearing I could not afford the cost of liability Insurance. Now being a third-class petty officer, I felt I could manage the operating costs that an automobile would require. Having "wheels" made an enormous difference in my situation. I could now get out and around, visiting relatives in the Bay area, and of course my grandparents who spent summers in Yosemite National Park. Our training included temporary assignments to Yuma, Arizona, and" carrier quals" aboard *Enterprise*, which at that time was home ported in Alameda, California.

After a short trip back to Albuquerque to leave my car at my mother's house, I returned to Lemoore to finish packing and head for Alameda to board *Enterprise*.

At that time, the *USS Enterprise* was the largest and only nuclear-powered aircraft carrier in the world. After serving on the *Ticonderoga*, a WWII vintage carrier, we thought we had died and gone to heaven. Four catapults instead of two. An airwing that included two squadrons of F4s, one squadron of A6s, replacing the A1 propeller-driven Skyraiders, and various other aircraft equipped with the latest in electronic evasion and detection equipment. Personnel accommodations were a welcome upgrade. No more "open berthing" on canvas bunks, but private enclosed bunks with each one having its own air-conditioning vent. We had joined the big leagues.

At an appropriate low tide, on November 19, 1966, we slipped under the Golden Gate Bridge and headed for the "Western Pacific" via Hawaii. At that time, the *Enterprise* Island structure was tall enough that a low tide was required to get under the Golden Gate Bridge. Several years later the *Enterprise* went through an extensive yard period where the Island structure was shortened so she could leave port at any tide, thus avoiding the risk of being trapped in San Francisco Bay.

Hawaii was a repeat of the squadron's visit the previous year. Operational Readiness Inspection, loading provisions, a few evenings on Waikiki before heading west.

We arrived in Subic Bay, Philippines, on the 8th of December for a six-day port call. Being a nuclear vessel, we knew that we would not be welcome in Japan, meaning we would be seeing a lot of Subic Bay on this deployment. Thus, we dug in and tried to enjoy some of the activities available on the naval base. Dungaree Beach and Grande Island provided some wonderful snorkeling, swimming, beer drinking, and sunburn opportunities. With a ship's complement of over 4,000 sailors, the adjacent town of Olongapo could become saturated quickly.

On December 14th we left Subic Bay and headed for Vietnam and another Christmas at sea. We were honored with the visit of Cardinal Spellman.

It was announced that he would perform midnight mass in the hanger bay for all interested personnel. I was not a Catholic, but had a good friend who was, and he invited me to mass. Prior to midnight, this friend and I decided we would have

Figure 12: Cardinal Spellman Enterprise 1966

our own private Christmas celebration. We took stock of our available provisions. I had a big homemade fruitcake that my mother had sent me for Christmas; my friend had a quart of Canadian Club whiskey that he had managed to smuggle aboard. The celebration began! By the time midnight rolled around we were feeling no pain as we headed to the hangar deck for mass. I remember enjoying the service very much but fortunately, being non-Catholic, I could not partake in communion. I'm not sure I could have walked forward to the makeshift altar.

Christmas and New Year's came and went with various "stand downs" in combat operations to honor the Vietnamese religious holidays. We concentrated on aircraft maintenance and the cleaning of airplane surfaces to protect them from the corrosive salt air. The good news was that we didn't have to cope with the black-stack gas residue every morning, one advantage of the nuclear power plant. We used a waterless cleaner, like hand cleaner, and lots of rags in our relentless battle with corrosion control.

In early January 1966, we were preparing for another port call at Subic Bay that included a short transit to Manila for a three-day stay.

Just prior to leaving the line at Yankee station on January 14th, we were conducting a night mission on a target near the border with Laos. It was customary practice on night missions to extinguish all exterior lights on the aircraft except for the small white tail light when descending for the target. The illuminated white light on the tail allows the trailing aircraft to orient and follow the lead aircraft down to the target in the dark. On this two-plane mission, for some reason, one plane's white light was extinguished, causing the two planes to collide in midair. Both pilots ejected and reached the ground safely. With a "mayday" transmission to air-sea rescue, ASR, it was confirmed that the pilots, in separate locations, had landed in Laos, uninjured. Using their emergency survival radios, the downed pilots communicated with ASR and It was decided that the pilots would remain in place on the ground until daybreak when the rescue team would attempt an extraction.

At first light, two separate ASR helicopters were dispatched. Ltjg Karl Vogelgro was located and raised by cable through the jungle canopy safely to the helicopter overhead, which then headed for Danang. The second helicopter located LCDR Arthur Tyszkiewicz. The helicopter began raising him by cable through the jungle canopy and above when suddenly, for no explained reason, the cable broke, sending LCDR Tyszkiewicz crashing back into the jungle. Despite continuous efforts to locate and establish contact with the pilot, he was unresponsive. A ground team was dispatched but again was unable to locate him.

Within a couple of days, LTJG Vogelgro was returned to the ship, where he elected to resign from flight duties and was immediately "high lined" to a destroyer for reassignment. Meanwhile, as a disheartened squadron, we mourned our first causality of the deployment, and tried to enjoy liberty in Subic Bay and Manila.

We returned to the line after a great port call in Manila, and the grind resumed. Combat flight operations continued relentlessly through the spring of 1967. On the flight deck, I continued to assist the seven plane captains under my supervision. It seemed like there was always some challenge or event going on that required constant vigilance and full attention. I recall one day in particular. We were preparing for a launch, pilots had manned aircraft, engines had been started, and plane captains and pilots were conducting their last-minute adjustments and flight control surface functionality checks. One of my plane captains signaled to me that he needed assistance, so I ran over to his aircraft. Above the jet engine noise and heat, using sign language, he indicated that the landing gear safety pins could not be removed and stowed, one of the last duties of the plane captain prior to turning the plane and pilot over to the aircraft handlers for taxi. I ducked under the plane and confirmed that all three of the safety pins could not be removed. I immediately sensed trouble. I signaled for the plane captain to get the plane's access ladder in position. I patted myself down to make sure that nothing was loose on my person and signaled the pilot that I was coming up. Because the engine was running, and I was about to position myself directly in front of the engine intake, I had to be extremely careful and cautious. I proceeded to climb the ladder and leaned my head into the cockpit to confirm what I had suspected. The plane's landing gear handle was in the up position and the aircraft's landing gear were trying to retract, the only thing preventing this being the safety pins. I pointed the situation out to the pilot who immediately relocated the handle to the correct position. I returned to the deck, pins were removed and stowed, and the plane and pilot headed for launch. How the handle had come to be improperly positioned was never determined or discussed further. All persons involved just secretly acknowledged that we had "dodged another one" to live another day.

Short Timer with a Short Temper

By early March, I became a "short timer" with less than 100 days remaining on my enlistment, I started the countdown. This also gave rise to efforts by the Navy to entice me to reenlist. I began to receive a series of "shipping over lectures" with promises of reenlistment bonuses, choice of duty station, college education, etc. My response was firm, no! When asked why, I would answer, "bad liberty, bad chow, bad pay." I was asked to sign a statement to that effect, which I did. A couple weeks later, while in the line shack, the phone rang asking for "Coen." I answered and was instructed to report to the pilot's ready room in thirty minutes in the uniform of the day. I complied, going down to the berthing compartment and changing out of my flight deck gear and into clean dungarees. I arrived as instructed in the ready room to find the squadron commanding officer, CDR Peter Sherman, seated in the second row and PO1 McDaniel setting in the first row. I was instructed to sit beside him. McDaniel began by going through three volumes of binders, page by page that explained in great detail every opportunity available to me if I would just agree to an additional 6-year tour. With the CO seated right behind me, I listened politely and patiently until he was finished. He then popped the question, "Well, how about it. Interested?"

I replied no and again repeated my reasons, within earshot of Commander Sherman, the CO: bad liberty, bad chow, bad pay. Again, I signed a statement to that effect, and the Navy conceded that I was on my way out. To Commander Sherman's credit, he and the Navy made an attractive and valiant effort to keep me in the Navy. However, behind my cocky attitude, the real reason I wanted out was I wanted my freedom and independence back. I had struggled so hard to gain both from my father. I wasn't about to hand it over to the Navy any longer.

As a post script, on June 10, 1967, four weeks after I left the ship, Commander Peter W. Sherman did not return from an "Iron Hand" mission near Hanoi. It was assumed that he had been "tagged" by a surface-to-air missile, (SAM.) His status was listed as missing in action, (MIA.)

On October 17, 1973 he was officially listed as killed in action, (KIA.)

On January 16, 1991 the wreckage of his plane was recovered 45 miles offshore near Hon Me Island. His remains were confirmed on 14 April, 1991.

My "short-timer" attitude began to develop into a "short temper" as the remaining days ticked off. I recall one night up on the flight deck as we were preparing for a night launch, I was standing around with several other support mechanics awaiting pilots. Trying to make myself useful, I was checking over a plane that had just come up from the hangar deck after undergoing an extensive preventative maintenance check cycle. These checks required several days and involved disassembling most of the plane's critical components for inspection. At the conclusion of this cycle the airplane is flown by the squadron maintenance officer for a final flight-worthiness test flight prior to the plane being returned to "ready for flight" status. During my own inspection, I stuck my head up through the aft "hell hole," a maintenance inspection panel. As I shone my flashlight around, much to my dismay, I discovered a maintenance "special tool" used to tighten the tail section bolts had been left behind by some careless airframe mechanic. This type of oversight could easily jeopardize the safety of the aircraft and pilot. Infuriated, I grabbed the wrench and charged out of hell hole to confront the nearby airframe mechanic. I shoved the wrench in his face and proceeded to give him a stern dressing down. I then took the offending wrench and threw it over the side of the ship, into the darkness. Still fuming, I returned to the airframe mechanic and proceeded to slug him with my fist as hard as I could. Now this man was no punk. He outweighed me by at least 50 pounds and could have very easily picked me up and sent me over the side to join the wrench. For some reason, he did nothing. He just walked away, and the incident was never discussed. I have always felt fortunate that I actually survived that night. I certainly didn't deserve to.

Because I had joined the Navy when I was 17, they were contractually obligated to discharge me at my three-year mark on May 21st. Looking ahead at our operational schedule, it became obvious that I would have to be flown off the ship to get me back to the states by May 21st.

In late March, we cycled through Subic Bay and headed for a week in Hong Kong. Knowing my Navy tour was almost done, I took one more fling at shopping, making sure I had something for each member of the family back home.

Figure 13: Hong Kong 1967

By early May, Flight operations began to intensify. We began to fly "Alpha Strikes" more regularly. These were strikes that involved every flyable plane and pilot aboard being launched in a coordinated strike, usually against the bridges and railroads outside Hanoi and Haiphong. These were substantial-risk missions, and we were all on edge. While the strike was airborne, we would anxiously await their return aboard a vacant flight deck and hanger deck. During these conditions, we were unable to land the usual daily mail plane because we had so many planes out that by the time we had recovered all of them the catapults would be unavailable due to parked aircraft. Thus, we would be unable to turn the mail plane around in any reasonable amount of time. This was significant because the departing mail plane would also leave with personnel that were leaving the ship due to emergency leave, reassignment, or discharge.

Around mid-May, we had been flying Alpha Strikes daily for over a week and had been unable to land the mail plane. They would fly by, we would wave, and hope that the next day might bring mail. Luggage was beginning to stack up in the Island structure as the number of people, officers and enlisted, needing to leave the ship began to grow. I had been told to pack my bags and add them to the growing stack and stand by for the next available mail plane. This went on for me for about three days when suddenly I was summoned to the flight deck. I was now considered "hot cargo" because of my looming required discharge date, they were anxious to get me on my way. A mail plane had been able to land to the carrier *Bonhomme Richard*, several miles away, and they had an extra seat. Suddenly I had been moved to the head of the line. They threw me and my bags aboard the helicopter and off we went to join up with the "Bonnie Dick." I was immediately hustled aboard the waiting mail plane, strapped in, and took a "cat shot"—catapult launch. I was on my way to Subic Bay Philippines.

I spent one night in the transit barracks at Subic before taking a bus over the mountain to Clark AFB, outside Manila. I hooked up with my buddy Roger, who had left the ship a few days earlier. He had become a permanent fixture at the enlisted men's club for several days and was in bad shape. That evening we boarded a contracted commercial 707 filled with service personnel and their dependents and headed for Travis AFB, California via Tokyo. I will never forget that night when we landed to refuel at Tokyo. They let us off the plane for a few minutes and I wandered around looking for fresh air. Outside on the tarmac, Army MPs with guard dogs stood watch over several hundred coffins stacked four high. I was grateful to be alive and going home. I had seen enough.

Roger and I spent a week at Treasure Island Naval Station as we processed out. We had one last meal together in San Francisco before flying to our respective homes the next day.

In May 1967 San Francisco was a hotbed of antiwar protesters, so the Navy had advised us not to travel in uniform. I was flying home on TWA, military standby, which required that I travel in uniform, so I took my chances. I recall landing in Albuquerque and being in a big hurry to deplane when a lovely stewardess stopped me. I was blocking the isle when she began asking me about my campaign ribbons. Self-consciously I explained each one, which she made a big deal of. The waiting passengers behind me responded with a welcome applause. She then let me off, wishing me well! Ed, my mother, two brothers, and a sister where there to meet me. We traveled home, and I took off my uniform for the last time.

I had been home about three weeks when I started to feel ill. I was having stomach pains, and of course the startle response and hypervigilance that I had acquired on the flight deck was still very obvious. I had been told that if I required medical attention within 90 days of separation that I should report to the nearest VA hospital. I did so in Albuquerque, and after a couple days of testing I was diagnosed with "anxiety reaction," stomach ulcers, and high-frequency hearing loss. Those many months of living off little sleep, adrenaline, caffeine, and nicotine had caught up with me. The VA prescribed Mylanta to control stomach acid and sent me on my way.

7

THE AFTERMATH

Following my release from the Navy in 1967, I set about doing what most newly discharged veterans did: I tried to find and make a new life. For the first time in my life, I was mostly "free." The world was my oyster!

During the last 8–12 months of my Navy tour, I began to set my sights on getting a college degree. I had promised myself that never again would I be subject to discrimination for want of a piece of paper. At that time, in the military, a college degree was everything, the difference between officer and enlisted. I was going to get one! Beyond that, I was interested in obtaining reliable income, securing female companionship, and starting some type of family life.

Following my arrival back home in Albuquerque, New Mexico, I had arranged for a temporary summer job assisting my stepfather in his job as the maintenance supervisor at the Casa Grande Lodge. I had recently been accepted at Northrup Institute of Technology in Englewood, California, and planned to relocate there for the fall term. I was planning on studying aeronautical engineering and was counting on receiving financial assistance from my G.I. Bill entitlement.

As I set about enjoying my new-found freedom, and summertime in New Mexico, I met Linda, a charming young lady who was also a summertime employee at the Casa Grande Lodge. At that time, she had just completed her sophomore year at the University of New Mexico. It wasn't long before a romance developed.

After a couple of months' courtship, we both began to consider the looming fall. She wasn't planning to return to UNM that fall for financial reasons. Instead she was planning to return to her home in Farmington, New Mexico, and enroll in the local branch of New Mexico State University.

As the date for separation began to loom, we both decided that rather than go our separate ways, we would marry, which we did. After a short honeymoon, we then packed my car with all our earthly belongings and headed for California.

Unfortunately, getting my G.I. benefits started was not that simple. By late December 1967, I had yet to receive my first check. To survive, Linda had gone to work, and I was working evenings at a local filling station. In desperation, we gave up on California and moved back to Albuquerque, where I could enroll at UNM and pay in-state tuition. Linda secured employment, choosing to postpone the completion of her college education.

Over the next four years, I managed to secure a series of part-time jobs that met our financial needs as supplemented by the GI Bill Education allotment. Additionally, Linda was able to return to her studies at UNM.

In 1971, Linda and I graduated from the University of New Mexico, Linda with a BS in education and I with a BBA, having switched from the engineering curriculum after two years. I felt very strongly about Linda finishing her education. In the event something happened to me, I believed that was the best insurance policy I could provide. The year 1971 also brought the birth of our son, Scott.

Unfortunately, in 1971 college graduates were long on supply and short on prospects. I had worked part-time for the previous two years for a local underground utilities contractor, so I decided to leverage that experience and went to work full-time in the construction industry. I found that with my pre-engineering technical course work, combined with my business degree, there was a niche.

We relocated to Linda's home town, Farmington, New Mexico, where I found supervisory employment with Fairchild Semiconductor. Fairchild was operating an electronics component assembly plant on the Navajo Indian Reservation at Shiprock, New Mexico.

After three years, and the birth of our daughter, Dawn Michelle, we relocated to California, where I could take advantage of adult night school opportunities and complete an MBA program. During this time, I found employment with a large international engineering services company and decided to follow the cost-engineering profession.

With a wife and two small children in tow, I began to develop my professional career. My wife, who had completed her elementary education degree, remained at home with the two children. Opportunities for career advancement took us to Pittsburgh, Pennsylvania, and then on to Quebec, Canada, as I developed my construction management experience. We returned to Farmington, New Mexico, in 1979, where I was employed as a cost engineer working on the construction of two large coal-fired electric generating stations. In 1982, my eagerness to "get ahead," and impatience, led me to go out on my own and start my own consulting business. By 1982, our children were 8 and 11 years old, nearing high school age. My wife had remained at home during their school years. During this period, I continued to suffer from hypervigilance, irritability, restlessness, depression, emotional numbness, sensitivity to noise (startle response) and an aggressive/angry disposition. Family and friends blamed it on caffeine and kept that out of reach whenever possible. My doctors began prescribing valium and other assorted antianxiety drugs.

Professionally, I was doing well—a respected member of the community, active in several civic organizations, and my business was growing. At home things were not as successful. Marital tension was high as my wife and I tried to reconcile differing life dreams and expectations. In retrospect, as I reflect upon this period, I believe I was experiencing classic PTSD symptoms and those symptoms were having a negative effect on my marriage.

Male Veterans with PTSD are more likely to report marital or relationship problems, higher levels of parenting problems, and generally poorer family adjustment than Veterans without PTSD. Research has shown that Veterans with PTSD are less self-disclosing and expressive with their partners than Veterans without PTSD. PTSD Veterans and their wives have also reported a greater sense of anxiety around intimacy. Sexual dysfunction also tends to be higher in combat Veterans with PTSD than in Veterans without PTSD. It has been posited that diminished sexual interest contributes to decreased couple satisfaction and adjustment.

Related to impaired relationship functioning, a high rate of separation and divorce exists in the veteran population (those with PTSD and those without PTSD). Approximately 38% of Vietnam veteran marriages failed within six months of the veteran's return from Southeast Asia. The overall divorce rate among Vietnam Veterans is significantly higher than for the general population, and rates of divorce are even higher for Veterans with PTSD. The National Vietnam Veterans Readjustment Study (NVVRS) found that both male and female Veterans without PTSD tended to have longer-lasting relationships with their partners than their counterparts with PTSD. Rates of divorce for Veterans with PTSD were two times greater than for Veterans without PTSD. Moreover, Veterans with PTSD were three times more likely than Veterans without PTSD to divorce two or more times.[24]

---

24 Partners of Veterans with PTSD: Research Findings–PTSD: National Center for PTSD–Jennifer L. Price, PhD & Susan P. Stevens, PhD

PTSD not only affects one's mental health, but it can negatively impact one's marriage as well. The symptoms of PTSD can create problems with trust, closeness, intimacy, communication, decision-making, and problem-solving often giving rise to the destruction of relationships. The loss of interest in social activities, hobbies, and/or sex can lead to one's partner feeling a lack of connection or being pushed away. A PTSD spouse can feel isolated, alienated and frustrated from the inability to work through the problems and help their partner. Partners may feel hurt or helpless because their spouse has not been able to get over the trauma. This may leave loved ones feeling angry or distant toward their partner.

The anger outbursts and improper impulses may particularly scare one's spouse. Verbal or physical violence can even occur, significantly adding to one's marital discord. Naturally, their spouse may become fearful of the abusive behaviors exhibited. They may feel pressured, tense, and even controlled by the survivor or by PTSD. Symptoms can be so severe and debilitating that spouses often feel like they are living in a war zone, in constant threat of danger, or may experience feelings of having been through trauma themselves.

Work and daily activities often prove to be a struggle as well for those diagnosed with PTSD and may contribute to higher rates of divorce and unemployment. Veterans who have been diagnosed with PTSD have reported significant marital difficulties. Studies have shown that nearly 50% of their marriages end in divorce and that they are three times as more likely to have multiple marriages end in divorce.[25]

I take full responsibility for the outcome of my marriage to Linda. Had I known about my PTSD and received treatment, who knows if the outcome would have been different? The reality is, discussions about PTSD and its symptoms were just emerging by the early 1980s. Meanwhile, for five years we had sought various therapies and counselors with negligible effect. Eventually, in 1985, I threw in the towel and filed for divorce after 17 years of marriage.

Thus, by mid-1985, I had a recent divorce, two wonderful children ages 11 and 14, and a struggling business to my credit. I once again found myself trying to start my life over, with the exception that this time the anxiety level was much higher as I now had significant responsibilities and obligations. I was no longer responsible for just myself, and I wasn't sure who I was or what I wanted to be. I guess you could call it a midlife crisis.

By 1990 I was remarried, with two new young stepchildren, a new residence in Colorado, my company disbanded, and several short-term employments to my credit. I had nearly doubled my responsibilities and stress level but had not

25 *Understanding PTSD and its Effects on Marriage.* Staci Lee Schnell, MSCS, LMFT, June 26, 2016

significantly improved my earning capabilities. Fortunately, my new wife, Donna, came with earnings capabilities of her own. She also came with a commitment to raise her two young children in a Christ-centered home. Up to this point, I had successfully dodged this issue since leaving the Navy, but it was now in my face! During the initial stages of my new marriage, I dutifully accompanied my wife and her two young children to church services at a Lutheran church (ELCA). In 1989, at the age of 43, alongside my 16-year-old daughter, I was baptized into the Lutheran faith.

The next 7–8 years were very tumultuous, both personally and professionally. As I was no longer self-employed, I found the transition to employee status very demeaning and unsatisfying. This led to multiple changes of employment. Dissatisfaction at work led to dissatisfaction at home with the resultant turmoil, tension, and unhappiness. As I reflect on this period, I recognize that I was a very angry and resentful person, and that resentment manifested itself in some very unpleasant ways. At work I was aggressive, belligerent, verbally abusive, and not a pleasant person to be around. It took very little to set me off, and heaven help the persons who did.

As I continued to try and redefine who I was, both personally and professionally—new family, no longer self-employed, and all the while dealing with the needs and antics of two developing adolescent stepchildren—cracks began to appear in my new marriage relationship. Following several separations of various durations, I encountered Promise Keepers (PK), a Christian men's group.

I watched for a year or so, and then decided to try a weekend meeting myself. The gathering was held during the summer at the old Mile High Stadium. There were several thousand men in attendance, and over the Friday evening and all-day Saturday program you couldn't help but feel the excitement and electricity. I was hooked. I began meeting with local Promise Keepers men for weekend retreats, small-group Bible studies, anything they had to offer. The theme was always the same: men keeping their promise to be good husbands, fathers, and sons. Men being accountable to other men and to God. Jesus was at the center, Scripture was the basis, and there was no liturgical protocol.

About this same time, I invested in a study Bible and made the commitment that I was going to read it cover to cover. By this time my employment career had stabilized. I was doing exciting work, traveling extensively, mostly internationally, and had significant professional responsibilities. Not to be deterred, I took my Bible with me and was often seen reading it in public, whether aboard an airplane or at breakfast from a jungle construction camp. It took me twelve months, but from Genesis to Revelation, I read every word.

I recall one specific Promise Keepers meeting in 1996 that I credit with having a profound impact on the future direction of my life. The meeting was scheduled for Friday evening and all-day Saturday. Several thousand men were in attendance. I was only able to attend the Friday evening session as I was scheduled to leave the next day for an extended assignment of several months in the jungles of Indonesia.

This particular Friday night session included a fiery presentation by one of the speakers who was preaching fire and brimstone. He yelled out to the crowd, telling the story of a young man that needed to get off the "freeway to hell," take the "exit to redemption," and "get back on the freeway to salvation." He went on with the story, telling how the young man had asked God to "send him a new wife," to which God replied, "What did you do with the one I gave you"? With that message burning in my brain, I caught the plane the next morning for North Sulawesi, Indonesia. My assignment was to assist with the construction, completion, and startup of a gold-processing plant in a remote part of the island. During those three months, isolated in the jungle, I had plenty of time to think. I came home with a changed attitude and commitment to my marital relationship.

My continued exposure and participation with Promise Keepers led me back to acceptance of my Christian faith, which I had abandoned 25 years previously. I became an active participant in the local ELCA Lutheran churches. I also studied and became a Stephen Minister and Stephen Leader, and ministered to several individuals who were experiencing life challenges of their own.

Professionally, despite my disposition, I was finally able to secure some very interesting, exciting, and meaningful employment. For the last few years of my career, I worked as a project management contract consultant. This enabled me to work outside the normal corporate "pecking order," and I was able to establish some autonomy for myself. I worked for some very large corporations on some extremely large projects, mostly international. I traveled extensively, all over the world, and was allowed to do my job without being concerned about my next promotion. I was mostly protected from corporate politics and could concentrate on "getting things done." As an engineering and construction project expert, I specialized in either getting projects started or getting them finished. I was well-known for my aggressive attitude, short temper, and abrupt manner. I was also well-known for results. This was the situation by the fall of 2004.

Subsequent Trauma

> *... previous exposure to traumatic events is associated with greater vulnerability to the PTSD effects of a subsequent trauma. ... the evidence of vulnerability to*

PTSD in adulthood in subjects who experienced childhood trauma is the first replication in a general population sample of previous findings based primarily on samples of Vietnam veterans[26]

November 2004 found Donna, me, and our two black Labrador retrievers, Meg and EV, testing out our new "mobile office." After considerable research and study, we had settled on and purchased a new travel trailer and tow vehicle. Recognizing the potential hazards of such equipment, we had spent considerable time researching the safety elements of both components and how best to match the two pieces of equipment for maximum personal safety.

We set out early in the month on a combination business and pleasure trip to test the fruits of our deliberations We intended to travel through New Mexico, Arizona, California, and Wyoming, visiting projects and clients as well as friends along the way.

We were on the last leg of the successful journey, leaving California on Interstate 80 and heading back to Colorado via Wyoming. As usual, the weather along the route was cold and windy, a winter storm having dropped significant snow over the higher elevations. We reached Salt Lake City by midafternoon of the first day, stopping at a heated truck wash to thaw the drain piping underneath the trailer to complete the winterization process. We decided to proceed on to Evanston, Wyoming, and spend the night in a motel as the trailer was now completely winterized.

The following morning, November 30, 2004, we set out on the final day of our trip across southwestern Wyoming, headed for our home in Colorado. The weather was clear, bitter cold—10 degrees, but without wind, a rarity for that region of Wyoming. Around 10:00 a.m., we were "pulling" the continental divide about 12 miles east of Wamsutter, Wyoming, the temperature having risen to 0 degrees, still void of any significant wind.

At this point, I should mention that after 37 years I was still experiencing significant symptoms related to my time in the Navy, serving on the flight deck. Startle response, hyperarousal, and hypervigilance were just a part of life for me. I often told people that I could "feel sound" before I could hear it, especially if it was coming from behind me. I didn't attend 4th of July fireworks events, fearing I would be lying prone on the ground during most of the show. Thus, I was always on "alert."

---

26 Previous Exposure to Trauma and PTSD Effects of Subsequent Trauma: N. Breslau, H. Chilcoat, R Kessler, G. Davis–*American Journal Psychiatry* June 1999; 156:6

As we continued up the grade I switched to the left lane of the divided roadway to pass a slow-moving 18-wheeler. About halfway through that maneuver, I heard a snap/pop sound coming from behind our truck. I immediately looked at my side mirror to find that the trailer had swung towards the left and was now almost 90 degrees out from the truck. This was followed by a violent swaying of the trailer, left to right, with such force it took everything I had to keep the truck traveling in a straight line. Meanwhile, we were still abreast of the 18-wheeler on our right side. About this time, Donna inquired if we were alright, to which I replied, no!

In a matter of seconds, the swaying trailer took control of the truck, first throwing us left, then right. I assume that the semi-truck driver was able to conclude what was going on and immediately began applying his brakes. Meanwhile with the trailer in full control, we traveled across the right lane, in front of the semi, our truck and trailer swapping ends so that we were now heading back west, and we were off the road on the right shoulder. At some point the trailer became separated from our truck and came to rest on its side. Our truck, no longer constrained by the weight of the trailer, nosed dived into the sagebrush and tumbled over, front first, landing back on its wheels. Except for two rear compartment windows, every piece of glass in our vehicle was shattered and gone. I recall as we were tumbling, looking out through the windshield as the ground loomed straight in, and thinking, this must be what it's like when you nosedive an airplane into the ground. Then everything went silent.

Once the noise and dust had settled, I ventured a glance over at Donna, expecting blood and trauma. She was just sitting there, looking forward. I asked her if she was alright, she replied "No." She then proceeded to tell me that she couldn't move her legs or arms. I immediately tried to open my driver side door, which wouldn't open, and I assumed it was jammed. I then proceeded to crawl out the door window, which still had a few shards of shattered glass remaining. I made my way over to the passenger side and tried to open Donna's glassless door. Fortunately, I was unsuccessful. I later realized that futile effort may have saved Donna's life. Had I been successful, I would have tried to move her and get her outside the vehicle.

I took a few moments to try and assess our situation. The semi-truck that I had been trying to pass was parked nearby and the driver came running over and asked if everyone was ok. I said yes, and he immediately got back in his truck and fled the scene. Several other passersby stopped and offered blankets for Donna, who was still seated in the cold.

I then began to check on our two dogs, who had been riding in the back along with boxes of wine and other assorted baggage. The dogs were laying among some broken wine bottles and other jumbled baggage, just panting, having, I'm sure, just experienced the ride of their life. About this time an officer of the Wyoming State Patrol arrived on scene, having been alerted by passing traffic CB radio.

I walked up to the officer and explained that there were broken wine bottles and wine scattered throughout the rear of the vehicle. I stated that I was a home wine maker and had brought some wine back from the California vineyards to sample. I volunteered to take whatever sobriety test he felt necessary to ascertain that alcohol was not a factor in our accident. He was very compassionate and considerate, showing his primary concern for Donna. He advised her to stay put and stay still; an ambulance was on the way.

As promised, the Wamsutter Emergency Ambulance arrived within minutes. The EMTs immediately assessed the situation. They were successful in opening the two front doors by pushing the "door unlock" button. They then crawled into the back of Donna's seat and proceeded to stabilize her head in a neck brace. In examining me they identified discomfort in my left ribcage.

The lead EMT advised me that they were going to transport Donna to the hospital in Rawlins, Wyoming, about 50 miles further east, and that they would be leaving in 10 minutes. They advised that I should also submit to the trip and hospital examination. I protested as I was concerned about what was going to happen to our dogs. The state patrolman assured me that he would transport the dogs to a veterinarian hospital in Rawlins where they would attend to them until I was able to reclaim them. I submitted, we were both placed on gurneys, and we began our 30-minute ride to Rawlins, Wyoming.

The Rawlins Hospital was ready and waiting for our arrival. They immediately separated us and began intensive x-rays, CAT scans, and doctor's examinations. After what seemed like a couple of hours, we were reunited, still on hospital gurneys. Donna was minus her neck brace and it looked like we might be released soon. Wrong! The lead doctor came running out of the x-ray lab instructing the staff to get the neck brace back on Donna and further stabilize her spine as "she was going on a plane ride." Flight for Life in Denver had been notified and was in route. It took about 45 minutes for the hospital to prepare Donna for transport, and then she was reloaded on the ambulance and transported to the Rawlins Airport to await arrival of Flight for Life. I called our local church pastor, in Evergreen, and she agreed to meet Donna at the hospital.

The attending physician advised me that he believed I had a couple of cracked ribs; he gave me some Advil and released me. The state patrolman was waiting as I exited. He advised me that the wreckage of our totaled truck and trailer was being taken to Wamsutter and our dogs were safe in the local animal hospital.

Dealing with our Injuries

My first concern was having a friendly face to meet Donna at Craig Hospital in Denver upon her arrival. Next, how was I going to get to Denver myself, some 250 miles away? I inquired about the availability of rental cars and found that none existed. I called our daughter, Dawn Michelle, who lived in Denver, and asked her to rent the largest SUV she could and immediately head for Rawlins. I found a local car dealer willing to rent me a used car for the day so that I could go back to Wamsutter and retrieve my glasses, our luggage, and several boxes of business papers including blank check stock. I traveled back to the "wrecked car lot" in Wamsutter, where I scrambled to retrieve as many of our personal belongings as I could from the truck. I would have to return another day for the stuff in the trailer.

As I was driving back to Rawlins to meet Michelle, I started to reflect on the day's events as I drove thru the quiet dead of night. I began to remember the chain of events that led to the accident, none of which made any sense to me. I then began to recall the sound of the pop, but further remembered the subsequent sound of a dragging chain. I instinctively knew that the sound was coming from the area around the equalizer/sway control hitch that connected the trailer to our truck. I began to immediately suspect a failure in the hitch/sway control/ equalizer components. However, I would have to put that investigation off for a later date. For now, I was concerned about meeting up with Michelle, transferring our belongings from my rental car to Michelle's rental car and picking up our two dogs.

About 8:00 pm Michelle and I met in Rawlins, where we transferred baggage and returned the car I had rented from the car dealership. The state patrolman had told me where he was going to leave Meg and EV, so we ventured over to the veterinarian hospital. The vet was very friendly but reserved. She told me that the dogs were resting quietly, had eaten lightly, and had taken water. She then proceeded to tell me that Meg was not walking well, and she was very worried that she had suffered some type of spine injury. She suggested she see our local vet immediately. Reunited, I carried her to the SUV that Michelle had rented. The vet wept as she said goodbye; I believe she feared the worse for Meg.

Neither Michelle nor I had eaten all day, so we decided to visit the local burger joint before starting our drive back to Denver. Prior to going into the restaurant, I was sitting in the front seat when I began to shake violently, all over. Michelle became very concerned and ran into the restaurant to get something for me to drink (caffeine/coke) and something to eat. After several minutes, the shaking subsided and I could breathe normally. I have long afterward attributed this reaction to events as a severe "adrenalin crash."

With Michelle driving in the dark for several hours, we arrived at our home in the foothills west of Denver at about 1:00 am. I carried the dogs inside and made Meg as comfortable as possible. Leaving an exhausted Michelle in charge, I headed down to Denver and Craig Hospital to see how Donna was faring.

Arriving at the hospital, I found our son Mark attending to Donna, who was barely awake with her torso elevated and her neck in a serious neck brace. We spent a few minutes getting each other caught up. As I recall, Donna related that she had a very competent neurosurgeon in charge of her case. She had been in various stages of examination and x-rays since her arrival and they were confident that she had a neck injury that would require surgery. The trauma team wanted to allow the neck fracture to stabilize for a few hours before planning the next stage. She was expecting further news in the morning. We agreed that Mark would remain with her for the remainder of the night, I would go home and try to get a few hours of badly needed sleep and return first thing in the morning.

Back at the house, the dogs were settling in, but it was oblivious that Meg was not right. It appeared that she had something wrong with her back and was having trouble standing and walking. The next morning, I called Dr. Manobla, our veterinarian, and explained our situation. He suggested I bring Meg in and leave her, so they could watch her and do x-rays, which I did while in route to the hospital to see Donna. By midday, Dr. McVickers, the neurosurgeon, advised us that Donna had an incomplete quadriplegic spinal cord injury that would require a C4/C5 fusion, anterior and posterior, to stabilize and repair the injury. He proposed to do the surgery the next afternoon. Mark and I made plans to tag team over the next 24 hours so that one of us was always present with Donna and that I would be there for the surgery the next afternoon.

Meanwhile I received a call from Dr. Manobla concerning Meg. He believed she had a compressed vertebra that was pinching a nerve. He further believed she would require spinal surgery to separate the vertebra and insert a spacer to relieve the pressure and compression. The surgery would need to be done by an outside facility, VRCC, that specialized in treating animal trauma cases. I proceeded to retrieve Meg from the vet's office and began the process of scheduling Meg for her spine surgery, which was to be done in the next few days.

December 2, 2004, at 2:00 p.m., Donna underwent surgery at Craig Hospital to repair her spinal cord injury. Several hours later, Dr. McVickers met with me and advised that all had gone well, and that Donna was resting in recovery. She was released to come home two days later. I then proceeded to have Meg's surgery, which also went well and was a success.

I now had two post-spinal-cord-surgery patients under my care at home, both of whom were very cooperative. The convalescent period for both Donna and Meg lasted through most of the month of December, with Donna still in a neck brace. I was busy trying to get our business stabilized and moving forward. Stress was high, and we were exhausted, but both patients were healing rapidly as we tried to look forward to celebrating the Christmas holiday.

PTSD Takes Control

A couple weeks into the new year, 2005, I began to hit a brick wall. I had developed a very distinct stutter, became very light sensitive, along with increased hypervigilance and startle response. When I found myself alone, sitting in the dark at night, trying to wind down from the stress of the day, I began to experience intense emotions. It was like someone had taken my "trunk of life" and turned it upside down, scattering all the contents over my head and on the ground. I began to review memories of old friends and family and felt like I was meeting each one of them again and "repacking my memories" in my closely guarded trunk. Some of the memories stirred up intense emotions; I found myself sitting in the dark of my nearby forest, crying as I spoke out loud to each one of these people individually. This process went on for a couple weeks until I decided to visit my primary care doctor.

She started by giving me a complete physical to make sure that the cracked ribs were all I had suffered from in the wreck. Finding nothing exceptional, she referred me to a local psychiatrist. Within a couple of weeks, I was able to get an appointment.

Following a lengthy interview, the psychiatrist referred to her DSM-V book and advised me that she believed I was suffering from PTSD. At that point, I had no idea what that was, but as she began to tie my military-service-connected "anxiety reaction" with the recent traumatic rollover accident, pieces began to fall into place. She readily admitted that she did not have the appropriate experience to deal with my case but gave me several relevant referrals.

Thus, began a seven-year odyssey of trial-and-error diagnoses and treatments, by multiple practitioners, to try and establish some sense of normalcy and functionality. After 45 years, the PTSD issue was now on the table and could no longer be ignored.

8

TREATMENT

In 2005, as the dust began to settle and the physical injuries resulting from our vehicle accident began to heal, we continued to sort through the wreckage to try to establish the likely cause of the accident. I felt very strongly that there had been a structural failure in the hitch equalizer sway control mechanism. After considerable searching and examination, I became convinced that a bolt holding the left side sway control torsion bar bracket had failed, disabling the left-side torsion bar, allowing the right-side torsion bar to take control. This caused the violent and uncontrollable swaying that we experienced.

Legal Consequences related to the Accident

We began to consider the possibility of filing a lawsuit against the manufacturers of the hitch to assist with the medical costs and potential lifelong disability for Donna that appeared inevitable. In late 2005, after a lengthy period of interviewing plaintiffs' attorneys, we finally settled on a firm that had the experience and willingness to undertake the case.

The first order of business for our legal team was to establish our current mental and physical condition, as well as the prognosis for the future. Donna continued to suffer from a limited range of motion as well as neuropathic pain in her upper extremities. I was experiencing severe sensitivity to light, severe word search difficulty, and stuttering, to the point of being unable to speak. In addition, my emotional state was very unstable. Outward expressions of grief, anger, restlessness, and anxiety were a constant state of mind. I was vulnerable to "triggers" at any moment.

Our attorney immediately ordered a series of physiological exams for me that included lengthy cognitive skills and aptitude testing. The conclusion was that I was functioning at an 8th-grade level, though I was a person with a master's degree.

I was referred immediately to a series of psychiatrists and other doctors, who began to try and treat my symptoms with a combination of drugs and "talk" therapy. Most of the drugs where from the SSRI (selective serotonin reuptake inhibitor) family, which my body could not tolerate. This "trial and error" treatment process went on for several months, utilizing several different practitioners. A couple of the practitioners even tried other types of therapy including different versions of EMDR (eye movement desensitization and reprocessing) therapy. Nothing was effective in reducing my symptoms.

In mid-2006, while in a conversation with our attorney, he expressed the opinion that I had a brain injury. After much discussion, we agreed that I would undergo a brain SPECT scan at my own expense. The abstract of findings was as follows:

Clinical Overview: October 10, 2006

The patient is a 60-year-old, righthanded, right eyed dominant, married, Caucasian male with reported diagnoses of head trauma, post concussive syndrome and post-traumatic stress disorder. The patient reported chief complaints of stuttering, fatigue, headaches, irritability, insomnia, difficulty concentrating and making decisions, jumping from topic to topic, distractibility, problems with inattention, cognitive processing, short term memory, and anxiety....

Brain SPECT Imaging Impressions–Established Indications:

Brain SPECT imaging was performed at baseline and during a concentration task. Significant findings in the established indications category are most consistent with the following:

- *Probable Traumatic Brain Injury*
- *Diffuse Cortical Hypoperfusion*

Brain SPECT Imaging Impressions–Emerging Indications:

Brain SPECT imaging was performed at baseline and during a concentration task. Significant findings in the established indications category are most consistent with the following:

- *Suggestive of an Anxiety-Related Disorder*
- *Suggestive of a Mood Disorder/Depression*
- *Suggestive of a learning/Language Disorder*

Recommendations for Emerging Indications:

Consideration might be given to the use of appropriate anxiolytic agents.

Consideration might be given to appropriate combination of pharmacotherapy and/or appropriate cognitive behavioral therapy guided by the physician's assessment of patient's specific need. The patient is already being treated with antidepressants.

Consideration might be given to a comprehensive neuropsychological/ psychometric and/or language processing assessment to identify specific learning difficulties. Based on the results, a specific neuro-educational/ rehabilitation program might be developed.

Moving on with our Lives

Throughout 2006 and most of 2007, Donna and I continued with the operation of our business, interspersed with continued medical and, for me, psychological treatment. My employment responsibilities required very little interaction with other people and were performed as solitary efforts and occasional travel.

In late 2007, I was personally engaged as a project management consultant for a major, multiyear construction project that required extensive interaction with a large project team spanning several large engineering and construction organizations.

During this period, we were successful in resolving all the legal remnants of our accident and further treatment of my medical issues where put on hold. In retrospect, this was a very trying and emotionally draining period. I quickly developed a reputation for being aggressive, explosive, abusive, and angry. Again, in retrospect, I can only ask forgiveness of all the individuals that I verbally abused during this period.

In late 2010, for my part, I completed my assignment successfully and returned home determined to discontinue further active employment. As I evaluated the previous three years, I realized that I still had a very serious mental health problem that I needed to address. As I undertook the assessment, I reconsidered the first diagnosis in 2006 of PTSD. The pieces of the puzzle began to fall into place.

In February of 2011, I contacted the Veterans Administration, requesting a reevaluation of my 1967 anxiety reaction diagnosis. The initial interview, by an outside contracted psychologist, was very painful as he was very skilled at pulling all my "triggers." At the conclusion of the interview, he closed the file and leaned over the desk and told me, "George, you don't have to live the rest of your life like this." I asked him for advice on assistance outside the VA as I knew the VA was going to be a lengthy process. He later emailed me a list of practitioners that he knew who had some experience with combat-related PTSD.

To the credit of the Veterans Administration, they acknowledged my previous condition and scheduled a series of psychiatrist sessions while my overall reevaluation was underway. While I only got to meet with this doctor for a couple of sessions, he proved to be very informative. This was the first time that I had a member of the medical profession address the issue of subsequent trauma. He described the typical chain of events this way: "Veteran comes home, feels different, maybe it's PTSD, but shrugs it off by trying to manage it himself. Life goes on with difficulty. Time passes and then, for some people, a significant event occurs. He busts up a bar, or wrecks his car or motorcycle, which results in trauma of some version. At this juncture, the veteran may begin to notice an increase in the severity of the previous PTSD symptoms. Potentially several years will have passed, but now the symptoms are significant enough for him to seek treatment."

From these conversations, I began to make some sense of my situation. Unfortunately, the case load of this particular psychiatrist would not accommodate a long-term relationship, so I began to seek outside mental health support. I now understood the basis of my problem and was better equipped to go about finding a solution outside the VA.

Eventually, my search led me to a speech therapist to begin learning biofeedback techniques to help with my stutter and word search difficulties. She was especially helpful as she had been the victim of a mailbox bombing in the 1960's and had suffered significant physical and mental trauma herself. She was a person who understood trauma on a personal level. Besides her very helpful therapy, she referred me to a local doctor/pharmacologist who specialized in the use of "off label drugs" in very small doses to address specific needs. He proved to be the answer to my inability to tolerate the SSRIs.

As part of the work with my speech therapist, I found that I was able to carry on a conversation by closing my eyes and shutting off all outside distractions or other sensory inputs. In late 2011, my speech therapist recommended that I have a Quantitative EEG, or brain mapping study. A QEEG brain map (or "Q" for short) enables the doctor to see the patient's unique pattern of mental strengths and weaknesses—areas of the brain where there is too little or too much activity, and areas that are not coordinating their activity the best they could. Once the doctors see the reason for the patient's struggles on a brain level, they can create a neurofeedback training program to help resolve it.

A synopsis of the findings and interpretation of my EEG include the following: ".... findings suggest a hyperaroused cortex, such as can be seen in hypervigilant individuals and those with anxiety-spectrum complaints."

I continued to try and find someone who had experience with my condition. In the process, I discovered the Army's "Warrior Reset Program." While I was not eligible, no longer being on active duty, I became intrigued with their protocol. One of the key parts is the use of hyperbaric chamber therapy. I found a local facility and discovered that they had an anonymous donor who was financially supporting veterans in need of this therapy. I gratefully accepted and underwent the 40-session protocol that lasted thru March of 2012.

In May of 2012, I received notice from the Veterans Administration that they were adjusting my disability rating to more accurately reflect my present condition. My legal advocate, The Disabled American Veterans, was not satisfied. They suggested that I ask for a review and submit some additional compelling documentation. In the meantime, I began seeing a very competent Veterans Administration psychiatrist/pharmacologist with extensive experience in treating PTSD. He immediately took over my prescription drug program, and I began to experience some significant symptom relief.

In October of 2012, I received the results of my requested VA "decision review." I was eligible for physical/mental health treatment through the Veterans Administration. This was the start of my real road to recovery. Shortly thereafter, the Golden VA Clinic relocated to a newly constructed facility with a fully staffed, extremely competent mental health group.

I continued with regular visits to my VA psychiatrist as we worked with various alternatives of my medications to strike a balance between anxiety control and functioning alertness. By late 2014 my VA primary care physician and my psychiatrist agreed that I should also begin psychotherapy, concentrating on cognitive processing.

I was assigned to a Veterans Administration psychiatrist who specialized in geriatric cases but had no specific experience with PTSD. This therapy involved a one-hour session every week at the main VA facility in Denver. The sessions concentrated mostly on "relationship management." After about 12 months the psychiatrist advised me that she was leaving the VA and I would need to be reassigned. At that point, I was questioning the results and benefits from the previous 12 months, so I discussed my situation with my psychiatrist/pharmacologist. It was his suggestion that I visit the Boulder Veterans Center and schedule an appointment with "Michael."

On August 25, 2015, I met "Michael" at the Boulder Veterans Center for a preliminary meeting, which ended up lasting over two hours. We started by exploring each other's background and experience. It became obvious very early that he was the "real deal"—Army Ranger, Vietnam, Purple Heart, etc.

He told me about being inserted deep into enemy territory to set up an observation post overlooking a section of the Ho Chi Min trail. He and his men would be there for over a week observing North Vietnamese activity, and then reporting back, by radio, movements along the trail, which by then was much more than a trail. At the completion of their designated mission, they would then make their way back to a safe landing zone to be airlifted back to base camp. They were expected to deal with any resistance encountered along the way.

We eventually got down to the business of why I had come. I related to him that I had been doing psychotherapy for over a year and was having a tough time believing that I had accomplished anything. I related a frequent experience of mine when friends or associates would comment about some involuntary reaction I might exhibit, by saying, "Get over it, it's been 50 years". My question to him was, "How do you get over it and still remain loyal to the memory of those that were left behind?"

For me, his answer was profound! He said, "You must learn to separate the emotion from the event." He went on to explain that when a painful memory is recalled, ideally you would like to remember the event in full detail, without triggering the emotion that leads to pain. He further elaborated; "That is what successful psychotherapy should be about."

Needless to say, I was ecstatic. I had finally found someone who understood my situation. Unfortunately, he let the other shoe drop, by telling me that he was weeks away from retirement and would be unable to take my case. Though devastated, I was still anxious to resume therapy but was still in need of a therapist.

The Turning Point

In September 2015, on the advice of my VA primary care physician, I enrolled in a class being given at the Golden VA Clinic called "Rewiring Your Brain," taught by the clinic mental health director, Dr. Patricia Alexander. This turned out to be a turning point and a life-changing decision in my battle with the symptoms of PTSD.

In this class, Dr. Alexander began to explain the physiology of the brain in easy-to-understand, layman's terms. Key take-aways for me included things like the following:

- The sympathetic nervous system (SNS) is one of the two main divisions of the autonomic nervous system, the other being the parasympathetic nervous system (PNS).

- The autonomic nervous system functions to regulate the body's unconscious actions. The sympathetic nervous system's primary purpose is to stimulate the body's fight-or-flight response. It is, however, constantly active at a basic level maintaining homeostasis. The sympathetic nervous system is described as being complementary to the parasympathetic nervous system, which stimulates the body to "feed and breed" and to (then) "rest-and-digest".[27]

- Treatment of complex trauma resulting from multiple trauma and/or childhood trauma requires a much more complex type of treatment, and classic psychotherapy is mostly ineffective.

- When the flight-or-fight response is triggered, the brain stimulates the amygdala, which results in overproduction of cortisol and adrenaline, which in turn depletes all of the body's other hormones.

The class was once a week for seven weeks, and each of the above concepts was discussed in detail and whenever possible, practiced. For the first time in my long PTSD journey, I was finally beginning to understand the significance of my affliction, what I could change, and what I could not. The Rewiring Your Brain class had a recommended sequel, Riding Out the Storm, which I signed up for immediately.

Riding Out the Storm—Retraining the PTSD Brain was presented in one-hour sessions over a seven-week period. The subject material was the neurobiology of stress, tactics for calming the nervous system, and was presented by Christina Laird, LCSW also of the Golden VA Clinic mental health staff. Again, this was a life-changing experience that served to further open doors useful for my recovery.

Riding Out the Storm focused on further developing and practicing brain retraining skills identified in the previous Rewiring your Brain class. Key concepts included:

- The PTSD brain has a hyperactive amygdala (hot amygdala) even in a resting state, a smaller hippocampus (learning and memory impairment), and fewer serotonin receptors.

---

27 Sympathetic Nervous System - Wikipedia

- Nonpharmaceutical treatment strategies include:
  - Retrain the brain
  - Activate some parts of the brain (cortex—here and now, self-awareness)
  - Quiet other parts of the brain, amygdala
  - Rewire: strengthen or weaken connections of brain cells (healthy or unhealthy behavior)
  - Make new connections between brain cells (connect old memories with different ideas, feeling, behaviors)
- Nonpharmaceutical treatments techniques include:
  - Feed PNS (parasympathetic nervous system—Vagus nerve) information that tells the brain to activate SNS and quiet the amygdala (imagery, grounding, yoga)
  - Learn and practice new behaviors to rewire old circuits—connect in current ideas, feelings, behaviors, weaken old ones (skills, exercise)
  - Activate PNS to reduce damaging stress hormones like cortisol (breathing)

In short, PTSD is a disorder of information processing. The PTSD sufferer's traumatic memories remain active because the brain structures concerned with memory storage and language have shut down, leaving the individual "on alert" until these parts of the brain are reactivated. It usually takes around a month for the brain to repair the "blown fuse" in the hippocampal pathway so that the usual memory-processing mechanisms can come back on line. For some people, however, it takes longer. This difference could be due to a number of factors, including natural variations in the capacity of the hippocampal pathway, the occurrence of other traumatic events that subsequently slow the repair process, or continued activation of the amygdala even though the danger has passed.

An intriguing possibility suggested by recent research is that vulnerability to PTSD has its roots in the early years of childhood. During a period when the brain is still forming, a lack of parental care or other stressors can alter the neural systems responsible for cognitive-emotional processing of traumatic information, leading to a reduced hippocampal volume. One implication of this finding is that some people are more susceptible to PTSD than others because they file their memories away less efficiently. [28]

Following the three months that these two incredible Veterans Administration sponsored classes consumed, I made the decision to resume therapy with Dr. Alexander's group. She consented and assigned me as a patient of Dr. Laird.

---

[28] *What Doesn't Kill Us: The New Psychology of Posttraumatic Growth*, Stephen Joseph, Ph.D. Basic Books p.55

In June 2016, I began seeing Dr. Laird for one hour, on alternate weeks. Our goal was to begin EMDR (eye movement desensitization and reprocessing) therapy, focusing on the traumas experienced during my childhood. Dr. Laird followed the common EMDR protocol used by the Golden VA staff, focusing and following a pencil that was being moved horizontally, back and forth in front of my face. While focusing on the pencil, I would concentrate on a target memory that we had agreed upon, and then allow the "Float Back" process to lead my mind. Eventually the mind would settle on some other strong memory, which would be the next target iteration.

The desired results were consistent with "Michael's" thoughts on separating the facts from the emotion. At the end of a session I was able to recall, think about, and discuss previously painful memories, minus the emotional pain. The actual process closely resembles the "self-help" techniques discussed in Francine Shapiro's book *Getting Past your Past*:

Most symptoms, negative characteristics, chronic disturbing emotions, and beliefs are caused by the unprocessed memories that are currently stored in the brain. In order to make sense of a current experience, the perceptions (what is seen, heard, felt) have to link into our existing memory networks. When an unprocessed memory is triggered by similarities in the current situation, since the memory contains the distressing emotions, beliefs and sensations of an earlier time, we experience the world in a distorted way. Even though we may be 30, 40, 50, 60 years old or more, it's as if we are holding the hand of our young self, and it's telling us what to do. ..... the earliest unprocessed memory that sets the groundwork for a particular problem is called a "Touchstone Memory. [29]

If these pivotal Touchstone Memories are processed, many others that are associated in the same network will automatically change as well. Once the memories are stored appropriately, the old disturbing emotions, thoughts and physical sensations no longer arise. Instead, positive emotions and thoughts that go along with the feelings of "I'm worthwhile," "I can succeed" and "I have choices" can arise automatically. [30]

Dr. Laird and I continued weekly EMDR therapy sessions for the next 10 months, starting with recalling my earliest childhood memories and eventually ending with my graduation from Santa Fe High School and enlistment in the Navy. We progressed chronologically through my childhood, processing each stressful memory, one at a time. With each targeted event, Dr. Laird would methodically guide me through a "reprocessing" of negative cognitions (negative beliefs) that were influencing my perspective of current events or occurrences.

29 *Getting Past Your Past*, Francine Shapiro, PhD, Rodale 2012 p. 75
30 Ibid p. 90

By late April 2017, we had reached a bridge; my military experiences lay on the other side. I was feeling a sense of calm from our previous work and was thinking I might be able to "go it alone" without having to open the "military can of worms." We agreed to temporarily postpone further sessions and see how I would do. I then began work on developing this manuscript, something that had been on my mind for some time. The process of writing about my family and my life experiences was sometimes soothing, sometimes painful.

In late December 2017, I was feeling like my anxiety level was beginning to get out of control, so I called Dr. Laird for an appointment. She found time to see me the following week.

During the following six weeks, Dr. Laird continued to revisit prior topics, but by now I was more willing and comfortable with "digging deeper." We spent a lot of time with and without EMDR, exploring my deep-rooted feelings around the term "abandonment." I began to acknowledge the two sides of abandonment—being abandoned, and abandoning others.

Upon close refection, I found that abandonment was a huge psychological issue for me. Perceived early childhood parental abandonment on the part of my father. My own guilt feelings of abandoning my mother and siblings to join the Navy. And lastly, the inevitable feelings felt by many vets who left before the fight was over and abandoned buddies and those who would never come home!

We ultimately crossed over the bridge into the previously unexplored territory of my military service. It was a gut-wrenching experience, but a journey I'm glad I took. Dr. Laird and I agreed to take a break for a few months to let the newly discovered feelings settle in a bit.

Hope and Optimism

Prior to parting, she introduced me to a concept and term I had never heard before: Post Traumatic Growth (PTG)—hope and optimism. She further mentioned that there was a group of Vietnam vets that met at the Golden facility weekly to discuss this concept. It was led by Mr. Ron Biela, LCSW of the Golden VA Mental Health Clinic with 10–15 Vietnam vets participating. She further provided me with some research material on the subject of PTG. I was intrigued and immediately set about trying to learn more.

Post-traumatic growth (PTG) was developed by psychologists Richard Tedeschi, PhD, and Lawrence Calhoun, PhD, in the mid-1990s, and holds that people who endure psychological struggle following adversity can often see positive growth afterward. "People develop new understandings of themselves, the world they live in, how to relate to people, the kind of future they might have and a better understanding of how to live life", says Tedeschi. "PTG can be confused with resilience, but the two are different constructs."

"PTG is sometimes considered synonymous with resilience because becoming more resilient as a result of struggle with trauma can be an example of PTG—but PTG is different from resilience," says Kanako Taku, PhD, associate professor of psychology at Oakland University, who has both researched PTG and experienced it as a survivor of the 1995 Kobe earthquake in Japan.

"Resiliency is the personal attribute to bounce back," says Taku. "PTG, on the other hand, refers to what can happen when someone who has difficulty bouncing back experiences a traumatic event that challenges his or her core beliefs, endures psychological struggle (even a mental illness such as post-traumatic stress disorder), and then ultimately finds a sense of personal growth. It's a process that takes a lot of time, energy and struggle."

"Someone who is already resilient when trauma occurs won't experience PTG because a resilient person isn't rocked to the core by an event and doesn't have to seek a new belief system," explains Tedeschi. "Less resilient people, on the other hand, may go through distress and confusion as they try to understand why this terrible thing happened to them and what it means for their world view."

"There appears to be two traits that make some more likely to experience PTG," says Tedeschi, "openness to experience and extraversion. That's because people who are more open are more likely to reconsider their belief systems, and extroverts are more likely to be more active in response to trauma and seek out connections with others."

To evaluate whether and to what extent someone has achieved growth after trauma, psychologists use a variety of self-report scales. One that was developed by Tedeschi and Calhoun is the Post-Traumatic Growth Inventory (PTGI). It looks for positive responses in five areas:

• Appreciation of life

• Relationships with others

• New possibilities in life

• Personal Strength

• Spiritual change.[31]

31 Growth after trauma–Lorna Collier, *American Psychological Association*, November 2016, Vol 47, No. 10, page 48.

At the present time, the Veterans Administration, nationally, is under considerable pressure to establish quantifiable treatment metrics that measure treatment progress and success. This is known as Evidence Based Therapy (EBT) and is supported by entry and exit assessments that can substantiate movement towards "wellness."

According to Mr. Biela:

...the PTG treatment protocol differs significantly from the EBT-type therapies that are currently being mandated by executive management of the Veterans Administration.

1. *PTG doesn't follow the usual model of treatment of EBP/symptom reduction. Trauma isn't treated as an illness or as symptoms. The trauma of the War and the aftermath is treated as an important part of the veterans' history that continues to be a part of who they are today.*
2. *The first stage of the group involves openly talking about how they were and are affected:*
   a. *The effects of Trauma, War, the Aftermath of War as Seismic: the world is convulsed, changed.*
   b. *Surviving can result in a strongly negative relation to the world: disillusionment (the world is unsafe, untrustworthy), alienation (can't relate to others), overwhelming (can' t take it), loneliness (unanswered need for connection), guilt (it's my fault)*
   c. *Coming home often was a new part of the trauma.*
   d. *Expectations and needs: for welcome, love, honor, support, understanding*
   e. *Sense of betrayal*
   f. *The power of negative emotions and experiences: losing connection brings fears, hopelessness, frustrations, confusion, anger, worsening PTSD, adaptations that bring their own problems*
   g. *Changes in personality, identity, values*
   h. *Not talking about it: the "conspiracy of silence"*
   i. *Common experiences of coming back from Vietnam, emotional needs not addressed, downward spirals of emotion*
3. *We focus on what Post Traumatic Growth means, how it is cultivated:*
   a. *Finding personal wisdom, meaning, strengths within oneself, including from the past, surviving the war and downward spirals*
   b. *Positive relations to one's self, others, the world, the future*
   c. *Awareness of capacities, developing and using inner strengths: esp. Wisdom, Courage, Compassion for self and others, Optimism*
   d. *Making sense of one's past and present*
   e. *New appreciation of, feeling for life, beauty, moral excellence*

f. Reordering priorities

g. Creating positive emotional experiences with others

h. Making choices for you and your future is essential to creating Posttraumatic Growth

i. Choosing to focus on strengths, hope, your potential

j. Choosing based on your values, what you believe in: looking for new ways to change your life

k. Following through with action, commitment, help from others: creating new patterns and habits

l. A conscious choice to give to and receive from others

m. Choosing to love and accept yourself, smile or laugh at your imperfections, mistakes

n. Choosing to consider and decide what impact you can have on others, on the world

4. *There is no protocol that's followed because the session is treated as organically developing from the principles of PTG: members are provoked by what I present, their individual responses lead the discussion and follow-up practices between sessions relating to my focus on the principles of PTG for the individuals present.*[32]

My own experience, as related above, shows how different therapeutic approaches by therapists who are committed to quality care can be the key for combat veterans seeking treatment for PTSD and growth. Rather than a standardized protocol or manual, which the VA has been implementing for "evidence-based therapies," what I found effective were individualized applications of therapy. I was fortunate to be offered innovative approaches such as "Rewiring Your Brain" and "Post Traumatic Growth," which were offered by VA therapists who were not supported by the VA as an institution. The Golden Mental Health Clinic has recently experienced the resignations of several of its most senior therapists. Many of the clients of these departing therapists, who have experienced successful healing, are now being left in treatment limbo. The patients' feelings of loss and betrayal runs high as they anxiously await the arrival of replacement therapists and the implementation of "Standard Treatment Protocol" as dictated by "Big VA."

For the Vietnam veterans, the end is near. Our aging, war-weary population continues to fade into history. Behind us, however, is a whole new population with its own unique war casualties. Hopefully, as a nation, we have gotten smarter and these wounded men and women won't have to wait so long for adequate treatment.

---

32 Group: Post Traumatic Growth for Veterans of the Vietnam War: Ron Biela, LCSW- 2018

9

THE RECONCILIATION

The First Step

I have been to The Vietnam Veterans Memorial, "The Wall," in Washington DC three times. The last time was in 1997.

At the time, I was seeing a psychiatrist in Boulder, Colorado, regarding persistent issues of anxiety and depression and my inability to maintain a consistent focus on relationships.

The psychiatrist was a very unique therapist. The sessions were two hours long and he would tape record each session. At the end of the session, he would hand me the tape to listen to at a later time. I would often find myself, while listening, commenting in amazement, "I said that?" Just having the opportunity to revisit the sessions was worth the price of admission.

Inevitably, the conversations got to my military service, and the subject of "Men Left Behind." After several sessions, it was agreed that I needed to find some way to "memorialize" this experience. We decided that I would make another trip to the Vietnam Veterans Memorial and obtain rubbings of the names that were important to me. I was then going to construct an appropriate memorial, which now hangs in my own version of the Wall, in my den at home. I arranged to make the trip during the Memorial Day holiday, 1997.

Of course, Memorial Day at the Wall is a significant event. The Rolling Thunder Group was represented in full force, accompanied by thousands of other people, there to pay homage. I had two names, Tyszkiewicz and Sherman. I also wanted to visit the "Book" at the end of the wall, where names of persons were placed who gave their lives for the effort but for various reasons their death was not considered "combat related." Webster was in this category.

I had secured the necessary rubbing parchment and charcoal, and I knew the location of my two names. I made my way forward through the thickening crowd. Tyszkiewicz was within easy reach, and I quickly secured a very nice image. Sherman was another matter. His name was high on the wall, well out of my reach. I looked around and was able to attract the assistance of one of the National Park Service docents. She quickly obtained a ladder, took my rubbing instruments, and went to the top of the ladder to secure the image. When she completed the task and came down, I was eager to secure the paper and move on. "No not so fast," she replied. "You must first tell me about this man and who he was."

Stunned, I replied, "He was my commanding officer," and then went into complete "meltdown." She handed me the paper, and I turned around trying to leave through the crowd as quickly as possible—sobbing, with my face in my hands. The crowd parted, and I was allowed to exit with dignity.

I turned my back on my comrades for the last time and walked away.

While they, and many others, are still with me in memory today, and the pain is still very real, in the roll call of my heroes, "All are present or otherwise accounted for," and I continue to live my life.

That's how I chose to honor them. I believe they would have wanted it that way.

Preparing for the Ending

After several years of tweaking and trial and error, the pharmacological treatment of my PTSD condition seems to have stabilized. While I am still at risk of "triggering" by unexpected events around me, it is not as frequent. I am still susceptible to adrenaline "rushes," but control through awareness has helped.

At age 72, as I reflect on my own "Post Traumatic Growth Inventory," I have several successes worthy of note;

Appreciation of life. Reflecting on the past 72 years, I have been blessed with many wonderful things, including four children, nine grandchildren, and at present two great grandchildren. My children are all doing well with responsible careers and families of their own. My oldest son, Scott, recently retired from a 26-year career with the U.S. Air Force in ICBMs. Daughter Dawn has completed college and gone on to have a successful career in IT. Mark and Karen have successfully followed in their mother's footsteps with careers in surety and Insurance.

Relationships with others. Back in 2011, during my first encounters with the Veterans Administration Mental Health Group at the Denver complex, it was suggested that I join a Vietnam vets discussion group that met weekly to discuss issues of common interest. I immediately discarded that suggestion as I envisioned a group of "crusty gunny sergeants" getting together and "refighting the war." I was not interested. However, with my new research information in mind, I decided to reconsider the group session concept. I asked Dr. Laird if she could get me into one of the Golden Vietnam Vets weekly meetings. Within a week, I received a phone call from Ron Biela, inviting me to the next week's session of "The Group," Band of Brothers.

The following Tuesday at 1:00 pm I entered the designated meeting room and met 12–15 of the greatest, friendliest, and most genuine men that I have seen joined together in a long time. Many of these men had been attending these weekly sessions for many years. In some cases, Ron Biela had been their therapist. I was immediately made to feel welcome. The meeting started off with each man around the table introducing himself and giving a brief background description. All branches of service were represented; all had served in Vietnam sometime between 1964 and 1975. There was no pretense; each man had a story and had the scars, physical and mental, to substantiate it. For the first time since I had started down the treatment road, I felt truly emotionally safe. We had all "been there, done that"; no further explanation or justification was necessary. I was instantly among friends. We shared a common bond, and it was fun to ridicule each other and have a good belly laugh at the result. It felt good to be among true friends again.

Ron gently directed the meeting with introduction of scholarly material provoking discussion that was meant to encourage introspection of growth opportunities. I look forward to continued involvement with this group of gentlemen, true heroes all!

Spiritual change. Ironically, for me, spiritual change and development has occurred, independent of any guidance or effort by the Veterans Administration. Therapy sessions conducted by VA staff were always secular in nature. When I discussed this with Ron Biela he suggested that Spiritual issues were generally lightly touched and referred to as "Reverence." Based on my own positive experience with development of this domain, this seems like a missed opportunity.

My spiritual life has significantly changed over the last 4 years. In 2014, Donna and I decided to leave the Lutheran Church in favor of a newly formed campus of Flatirons Community Church in Genesee. As we began to grow with that congregation, we took advantage of several small-group retreats, Bible studies, and seminars.

As my faith journey continued, I found myself wrestling more and more with "trusting God"—did I really? As I began to consider "end of life issues," I became increasingly aware that I was having to loosen "control" of events around me. The more I pondered this circumstance and the results that were now "my life," I began to question, Was I ever really in control? and Where has God been all these years of my life?

As I continued to wrestle with my relationship with God, I found myself asking the question, "Could I really trust God with my total submission?" "Had he been there for me in the past, was he with me now"? The desire was there, but so was the doubt and hesitation. I longed for answers to the contradiction between God's goodness and human suffering. Central to that issue was the question, "why did bad things happen to good people?" By age 72, I had plenty of reasons to ask this question.

With my military experience having firmly influenced the development of my core beliefs, I was having significant difficulty reconciling a Faith Commitment with my past life experiences.

As I continued to grow with the new church community, I often heard stories and references to "The Crucible Project" as a significant men's weekend, offsite growth opportunity.

As I continued to explore my core beliefs, I found myself having to answer the question, what did I want for my soul? I defined "soul" as the spiritual or immaterial part of a human, regarded as immortal. I settled on "peace" as the answer—defining peace as freedom from disturbance, along with quiet and tranquility.

Finally, I surmised that to achieve peace in this sense, I would have to accomplish the following: give up feeling frustrated, betrayed, and abandoned; give up control; replace resentment with peace; and trust God. After much contemplation and introspection, I decided that I was ready, and I made the commitment to attend a Crucible weekend retreat.

To preserve the Crucible experience for future attendees, each participant commits to honor the pledge that "What happens at Crucible, stays at Crucible." For me, I will only say that the weekend experience was one of the most intense physical, mental, and emotional challenges that I have ever experienced. Yes, I wrestled with God and came to know him and how he had always been a part of my life, whether or not I acknowledged it at the time.

I came home at peace, knowing I could trust God to do the right thing with the remaining few years of my life. What more could I ask?

Prior to my Crucible experience if I had been asked to profess my statement of faith it would have probably gone something like this:

> For most of my life, God has been some mystical being out there that is somehow responsible for all things. In spite of all that, I'm still in control and responsible for short-term outcomes.
>
> The conflicting tension is the persistent presence of that "inner voice" that is often times in conflict with my actions.

Today at age 72, having completed Crucible, I would summarize my faith as follows:

> Jesus is the example of the person I should aspire to be.
>
> It's not about the destination; it's about the voyage. I need to be less concerned about the future and more concerned with the present. God has a plan for my life, but only the ending is made known to me and is certain. The path will be revealed to me in small increments. I just need to pay attention and listen.
>
> I believe that voice that is constantly talking to me over my shoulder is that revelation in small bits. I just need to listen and heed.
>
> God's intermediate destinations for me may not be consistent with my desires or expectations; however, I'm expected to obey! Terrible things happen to good people, thus the significance of the Cross and the Resurrection.
>
> I know God loves me and is with me!

The empirical literature points to a clear conclusion: spirituality is part and parcel of the human response to trauma and its resolution. Research indicates that spirituality can facilitate or impede PTG.[33]

Spiritual educators and leaders could provide an important service to their larger community by acknowledging spiritual struggles and normalizing these struggles as a commonplace and potentially valuable dimension of spiritual experience. By strengthening spiritual resources, recognizing the reality of spiritual struggles, and assisting people in the process of resolving these struggles, practitioners may be able to help people grow rather than decline through encounters with trauma. [34]

---

33 Handbook of Posttraumatic Growth - Research and Practice - Lawrence G. Calhoun and Richard G. Tedeschi Psychology Press p.132
34 Ibid, p.134

In the immortal words of G.K. Chesterton, when asked by a reporter what he would do if the risen Christ were now standing right behind him, Mr. Chesterton simply replied, "But he is."

10

THE SCIENCE OF PTSD

History of PTSD in Veterans: Civil War to DSM-5

In 1919 President Wilson proclaimed November 11th (the day World War I ended) as the first observance of Armistice Day, At that time, some symptoms of present-day PTSD were known as "shell shock" because they were seen as a reaction to the explosion of artillery shells. Symptoms included panic and sleep problems, among others. Shell shock was first thought to be the result of hidden damage to the brain caused by the impact of the big guns. Thinking changed when more solders who had not been near explosions had similar symptoms. "War neurosis" was also a name given to the condition during this time. During World I, treatment was varied. Solders often received only a few days' rest before returning to the war zone. For those with severe or chronic symptoms, treatment focused on daily activity to increase functioning in hopes of returning them to productive civilian lives. In European hospitals hydrotherapy (water) or electrotherapy (shock) were used along with hypnosis.

In World War II, the shell shock diagnosis was replaced by combat stress reaction (CSR), also known as "battle fatigue." With long surges common in World War II, soldiers became battle-weary and exhausted. Some American military leaders such as Lieutenant Gen. George S. Patton did not believe "battle fatigue" was real. Up to half of the World War II military discharges were said to be the result of combat exhaustion. CSR was treated using "PIE" (proximity, immediacy, expectancy) principles. PIE required treating causalities without delay and making sure sufferers expected complete recovery so that they could return to combat after rest. The benefits of military unit relationships and support became a focus of both preventing stress and promoting recovery.

In 1952, The American Psychiatric Association (APA) produced the first Diagnostic and Statistical Manual of Mental Disorders (DSM-I), which included "gross stress reaction." This diagnosis was proposed for people who were relatively normal, but who had symptoms from traumatic events such as disaster or combat. A problem was that this diagnosis assumed that reactions to trauma would resolve relatively quickly. If symptoms were still present after six months, another diagnosis was required.

Despite growing evidence that trauma exposure was associated with psychiatric problems, this diagnosis was eliminated in the second edition of DSM (1968). DSM-II included "adjustment reaction to adult life," which was clearly insufficient to capture a PTSD-like condition. This diagnosis was limited to three examples of trauma: unwanted pregnancy with suicidal thoughts, fear linked to military combat, and Ganser syndrome (marked by incorrect answers to questions) in prisoners who face a death sentence.

In 1980, APA added PTSD to DSM-III, which stemmed from research involving returning Vietnam War veterans, Holocaust survivors, sexual trauma victims, and others. Links between the trauma of war and postmilitary civilian life were established.

The DSM-III criteria were revised in DSM-III-R (1987), DSM-IV (1994), DSM-IV-TR (2000), and DSM-5 (2013) to reflect continuing research. One important finding, which was not clear at first, is that PTSD is relatively common. Recent data shows about 4 of every 100 American men (or 4%) and 10 out of every 100 American women (or 10%) will be diagnosed with PTSD in their lifetime.

An important change in DSM-5 is that PTSD is no longer an anxiety disorder. PTSD is sometimes associated with other mood states (for example, depression) and with angry or reckless behavior rather than anxiety. So, PTSD is now in a new category, trauma-and stressor-related disorders. PTSD includes four different types of symptoms: reliving the traumatic event (also called reexperiencing or intrusion); avoiding situations that are reminders of the event; negative changes in beliefs and feelings; and feeling keyed up (also called hyperarousal or overreactive to situations). Most people experience some of these symptoms after a traumatic event, so PTSD is not diagnosed unless all four types of symptoms last for at least a month and cause significant distress or problems with day-to-day functioning.[35]

---

35 PTSD: National Center for PTSD – History of PTSD in Veterans: Civil War to DSM-5, Matthew J. Friedman, MD, PhD

The Science Behind PTSD Symptoms: How Trauma Changes the Brain

After any type of trauma—from combat to car accidents, natural disasters to domestic violence, sexual assault to child abuse—the brain and body change. Every cell records memories, and every embedded trauma-related neuropathway has the opportunity to repeatedly reactivate.

Sometimes the alterations these imprints create are transitory, the small glitch of disruptive dreams and moods that subside in a few weeks. In other situations, the changes evolve into readily apparent symptoms that impair function and present in ways that interfere with jobs, friendships, and relationships.

One of the most difficult aspects for survivors in the aftermath of trauma is understanding the changes that occur, plus integrating what they mean, how they affect a life, and what can be done to restructure them. Launching the recovery process begins with normalizing post-trauma symptoms by investigating how trauma affects the brain and what symptoms these effects create.

The 3-Part Brain

The Triune Brain Model, introduced by physician and neuroscientist Paul D. MacLean, explains the brain in three parts:

- Reptilian (brain stem): This innermost part of the brain is responsible for survival instincts and autonomic body processes.
- Paleomammalian (limbic, midbrain): The midlevel of the brain, this part processes emotions and conveys sensory relays.
- neomammalian (cortex, forebrain): The most highly evolved part of the brain, this outer area controls cognitive processing, decision making, learning, memory, and inhibitory functions.

During a traumatic experience, the reptilian brain takes control, shifting the body into reactive mode. Shutting down all nonessential body and mind processes, the brain stem orchestrates survival mode. During this time, the sympathetic nervous system increases stress hormones and prepares the body to fight, flee, or freeze.

In a normal situation, when an immediate threat ceases, the parasympathetic nervous system shifts the body into restorative mode. This process reduces stress hormones and allows the brain to shift back to the normal top-down structure of control.

However, for those 20 percent of trauma survivors who go on to develop symptoms of post-traumatic stress disorder (PTSD)—an unmitigated experience of anxiety related to the past trauma—the shift from reactive to responsive mode never occurs. Instead, the reptilian brain, primed to threat and supported by dysregulated activity in significant brain structures, holds the survivor in a constant reactive state.

The Dysregulated Post-Trauma Brain

The four categories of PTSD symptoms include: intrusive thoughts (unwanted memories); mood alterations (shame, blame, persistent negativity); hypervigilance (exaggerated startle response); and avoidance (of all sensory and emotional trauma-related material). These cause confusing symptoms for survivors who don't understand how they've suddenly become so out of control in their own minds and bodies.

Unexpected rage or tears, shortness of breath, increased heart rate, shaking, memory loss, concentration challenges, insomnia, nightmares, and emotion numbing can hijack both an identity and a life. The problem isn't that the survivor won't "just get over it" but that he/she needs time, help, and the opportunity to discover his/her own path to healing in order to do so.

Throughout the brain several chemical and biological imbalances can present after trauma. Their effects are especially exacerbated by three major brain function dysregulations:

- Overstimulated amygdala: An almond-shaped mass located deep in the brain, the amygdala is responsible for survival-related threat identification, plus tagging memories with emotion. After trauma, the amygdala can get caught up in a highly alert and activated loop during which it looks for or perceives threat everywhere.

- Underactive hippocampus: An increase in the stress hormone glucocorticoid kills cells in the hippocampus, which renders it less effective in making synaptic connections necessary for memory consolidation. This interruption keeps both the body and mind stimulated in reactive mode as neither element receives the message that the threat has transformed into the past tense.

- Ineffective variability: The constant elevation of stress hormones interferes with the body's ability to regulate itself. The sympathetic nervous system remains highly activated, leading to fatigue of the body and many of its systems, most notably the adrenal.

How Healing Happens

While changes to the brain can seem, on the surface, disastrous and representative of permanent damage, the truth is all of these alterations can be reversed. The amygdala can learn to relax; the hippocampus can resume proper memory consolidation; the nervous system can recommence its easy flow between reactive and restorative modes. The key to achieving a state of neutrality and then healing lies in helping to reprogram the body and mind.

While the two collaborate in a natural feedback loop, processes designed for each individually are vast. Hypnosis, neurolinguistics programming, and other brain-related modalities can teach the mind to reframe and release the grip of trauma. Likewise, approaches including somatic experiencing, tension-and-trauma-releasing exercises, and other body-centric techniques can help the body recalibrate to normalcy.

Survivors are unique; their healing will be individual. There is no one-size-fits-all or personal guarantee for what will work (and the same program will not work for everyone). However, the majority of evidence suggests that when survivors commit to a process of exploring and testing treatment options they can, over a period of time, reduce the effects of trauma and even eliminate symptoms of PTSD.[36]

Childhood Physical Abuse and Combat-Related Posttraumatic Stress Disorder in Vietnam Veterans

> *Patients with a history of abuse may be vulnerable to the development of combat-related PTSD. Individuals abused in childhood may have acquired characteristic methods of coping with stressful experiences, such as emotional numbing, which may, in fact, make them more susceptible to subsequent trauma such as combat stress…. In other words, exposure to stress early in life increases the vulnerability to psychopathology in response to subsequent stressors, rather than having a protective effect. Studies of the neurobiology of stress suggest that exposure to stress early in life may result in long-term changes in neurobiological systems that are involved in the stress response.[37]*

The preceding paragraph can function as a short summary of my story. My PTSD is real, but it's more than a reaction to war experiences. My experiences of abuse in childhood caused me to develop coping and processing patterns that made me vulnerable to PTSD when experiencing trauma as an adult.

---

36 The Science Behind PTSD Symptoms: How Trauma Changes the Brain, Michele Rosenthal
37 Childhood Physical Abuse and Combat-Related Posttraumatic Stress Disorder in Vietnam Veterans, J, Douglas Bremner, et all. American Journal Psychiatry 150:2, February 1993

I pray that this book will not only help people understanding their own PTSD, but also make them aware of the effects of PTSD on people around them.

11

RESOURCES FOR FURTHER STUDY

Brain & Behavior Research Foundation. Frequently Asked Questions about Post-Traumatic Stress Disorder (PTSD). https://www.bbrfoundation.org/faq/frequently-asked-questions-about-post-traumatic-stress-disorder-ptsd.s

Bremner, J. Douglas, Penny Randall, Eric Vermetten, Lawrence Staib, Richard A. Bronen, Carolyn Mazure, Sandi Capelli, Gregory McCarthy, Robert B. Innis, and Dennis S. Charney. 1997. Magnetic Resonance Imaging-Based Measurement of Hippocampal Volume in Posttraumatic Stress Disorder Related to Childhood Physical and Sexual Abuse—A Preliminary Report. Biological Psychiatry 41(1): Jan 1.

Bremner, J. Douglas, Steven M. Southwick, David R. Johnson, Rachel Yehuda, and Dennis S. Charney. 1993. Childhood Physical Abuse and Combat-Related Posttraumatic Stress Disorder in Vietnam Veterans. *American Journal of Psychiatry* 150.

Breslau, Naomi, Howard D. Chilcoat, Ronald C. Kessler, and Glenn C. Davis. 1999. Previous Exposure to Trauma and PTSD Effects of Subsequent Trauma: Results from the Detroit Area Survey of Trauma. *American Journal of Psychiatry* 156(6): June.

Breslau, Naomi, Edward L. Peterson, and Lonni R. Schultz. 2008. A Second Look at Prior Trauma and the Posttraumatic Stress Disorder Effects of Subsequent Trauma. *Archives of General Psychiatry 65(4).*

Brunet, Alain, Richard Boyer, Daniel S. Weiss, and Charles R Marmar. 2001. The Effects of Initial Trauma Exposure on the Symptomatic Response to a Subsequent Trauma. *Canadian Journal of Behavioral Science* 33(2).

Cabrera, Oscar A., Charles W. Hoge, Paul D. Bliese, Carl A. Castro, and Stephen C. Messer. 2007. Childhood Adversity and Combat as Predictors of Depression and Post-Traumatic Stress in Deployed Troops. *American Journal of Preventative Medicine* 33(2).

"Can We Facilitate Posttraumatic Growth in Combat Veterans?" Richard G. Tedeschi & Richard J. McNally, *American Psychologist*, January 2011, Vol. 66, No. 1, 19-24

Cardona, Robert, and Elspeth Ritchie. 2018. Psychological Screening of Recruits Prior to Accession in the US Military. *Recruit Medicine*. Army Medical Department Center and School.

DeAngelis, Tori. 2008. Helping Families Cope with PTSD. *American Psychological Association* 39(1), Jan.

————. 2008. PTSD Treatments Grow in Evidence, Effectiveness. *American Psychological Association* 39(1), Jan.

Jenkins, Sarah. 2017. More Than Just Eye Movements: The Eight Phases of EMDR. https://www.goodtherapy.org/blog/eight-phases-of-emdr/

Kuo, Janice R., Danny G. Kaloupek, and Steven H. Woodward. 2012. Amygdala Volume in Combat-Exposed Veterans with and without Posttraumatic Stress Disorder. *Archives of General Psychiatry* 90(10).

L.G. Calhoun & R.G. Tedeschi (Eds.), *Handbook of posttraumatic growth: Research and practice (pp. 3-33). Mahwah, NJ: Erlbaum*

Lancaster, Cynthia L., Jenni B. Teeters, Daniel F. Gros, and Sudie E. Back. 2016. *Journal of Clinical Medicine* 5(11), Nov.

Lavallee, Sarah. 2012. Enduring Casualties of War: Delayed Treatment of Combat Stress in World War II Veterans. *Journal of History* 14.

Military Selection and Psychological Testing. 2010. http://psychologytec2010.blogspot.com/2010/04/military-selection-and-psychological.html

National Center for PTSD. History of PTSD in Veterans: Civil War to DSM-5. https://www.ptsd.va.gov.

————. Treatment of PTSD.

————. What Are the Symptoms of PTSD?

————. What Is PTSD?

Poole, Robert M. 2010. The Pathway Home Makes Inroads in Treating PTSD. *Smithsonian*. Sep.

PTSD and Vietnam Veterans: A Lasting Issue 40 Years Later. 2015. *Agent Orange Newsletter*. Summer.

Report on Preliminary Mental Health Screenings for Individuals Becoming Members of the Armed Forces. *Report on Section 593 of the National Defense Authorization Act for Fiscal Year 2016 (Public Law 114-92)*. U.S. Department of Defense.

Riggs, David S. Riggs, Christina A. Byrne, Frank W. Weathers, and Brett T. Litz. 1998. The Quality of the Intimate Relationships of Male Vietnam Veterans: Problems Associated with Posttraumatic Stress Disorder. *Journal of Traumatic Stress* (11(1).

Sareen, J., C. A. Henriksen, S L. Bolton, T. O. Afifi, M. B. Stein, and G. J. G. Asmundson. 2013. Adverse childhood experiences in relation to mood and anxiety disorders in a population-based sample of active military personnel. *Psychological Medicine* 43(1), Jan.

Shin, Lisa M., Scott P. Orr, Margaret A. Carson, Scott L. Rauch, Michael L. Macklin, Natasha B. Lasko, Patricia Marzol Peters, Linda J. Metzger, Darin D. Dougherty, Paul A. Cannistraro, Nathaniel M. Alpert, Alan J. Fischman, and Roger K. Pitman. Regional Cerebral Blood Flow in the Amygdala and Medial Prefrontal Cortex During Traumatic Imagery in Male and Female Vietnam Veterans with PTSD 2004. *Archives of General Psychiatry.* 61:168-176.

Shapiro, Francine. 2017. How EMDR Therapy Opens a Window to the Brain. *Brain World.* http://brainworldmagazine.com/how-emdr-therapy-opens-a-window-to-the-brain/, Oct. 1.

Sympathetic Nervous System. Wikipedia. Retrieved Dec. 15, 2017.

Volpicelli, Joseph, Geetha Balaraman, Julie Hahn, Heather Wallace, and Donald Bux. 1999. The Role of Uncontrollable Trauma in the Development of PTSD and Alcohol Addiction. CE-Credit.com, vol. 23(4).

What Doesn't Kill Us: The New Psychologist of Posttraumatic Growth by Stephen Joesh, Ph.D. (New York: Basic Books, 2011)

Woodward, Steven H., Janice R. Kuo, Marie Schaer, Danny G. Kaloupek, and Stephan Eliez. 2013. Early adversity and combat exposure interact to influence anterior cingulate cortex volume in combat veterans. NeuroImage: Clinical 2.

Yehuda, Rachel, and Linda M. Bierer. 2009. The Relevance of Epigenetics to PTSD: Implications for the *DSM-V. Journal of Traumatic Stress* 22(5), Oct.

Yehuda, Rachel, and Joseph LeDoux. 2007. Response Variation following Trauma: A Translational Neuroscience Approach to Understanding PTSD. *Neuron* 56, Oct.

Youssef, Nagy A., Kimberly T. Green, Eric A. Dedert, Jeffrey S. Hertzberg, Patrick S. Calhoun, Michelle F. Dennis, Mid-Atlantic Mental Illness Research, Education and Clinical Center Workgroup, and Jean C. Beckham. 2013. Exploration of the Influence of Childhood Trauma, Combat Exposure, and the Resilience Construct on Depression and Suicidal Ideation among U.S. Iraq/Afghanistan era Military Personnel and Veterans. *Archives of Suicide Research* 17(2).

Zaidi, Lisa Y., and David W. Foy. 1994. Childhood Abuse Experiences and Combat-Related PTSD. *Journal of Traumatic Stress* 7(1).